Understanding
The Old Testament

Understanding The Old Testament

An Introductory Atlas to the Hebrew Bible

Baruch Sarel

Carta, Jerusalem

Copyright © 1997
Carta, The Israel Map and Publishing Company Ltd., Jerusalem

This edition has been expanded from the original Hebrew edition.

Translated by Barbara Ball

The Scripture quotations in this publication are from the Authorized King James Version.

ISBN 965-220-364-5

Printed in Israel

Contents

List of Maps

(overleaf) The Valley of Aijalon.

Preface

Children hear their first Bible stories at home from their parents or grandparents, or in Sunday School from teachers whose names, too, are often biblical. As they grow older most children are introduced to Bible studies proper. Because of the vast scope of the work, such Bible studies usually concentrate only on selected books and chapters. These are often studied in depth and taught with great intensity or even by rote. Still, most adults end up remembering only a small portion of what they had learned: a few stories, prominent personages, or fragments of biblical passages. If asked to write down all that was remembered from hundreds of Bible lessons, sometimes it is doubtful whether all but a few pages could be filled, or if much accuracy could be retained.

How, then, despite the inexhaustible mine of information acquired, were all these hours of Bible teaching and study lost? One possible reason lies in the fact that the Bible is usually studied in a fragmentary manner, not within a comprehensive framework that is structured and organized from beginning to end. The importance of a structured framework may be somewhat exaggerated, but it can undoubtedly ease Bible study and make it more interesting and memorable. This Atlas provides just such a framework—a historical-geographical backdrop to the understanding of the Bible, providing the broadest background possible for placing the events and persons within a tangible framework of time and space.

We set forth the premise that the need for Bible study should not be subject to proof. The Bible is an inseparable part of Judaism, Christianity, and of Western culture in general. Remove the Bible from humankind, and all the cultures bound in Judaism and Christianity will lose the cornerstone of their foundations and a significant part of their meaning. Bible study, therefore, is a necessity.

Furthermore, the Bible reveals itself differently to different people, and can be studied in more than one manner. The Bible remains strong and firm despite the variant beliefs and extreme viewpoints ascribed to it, and, in this spirit, we present this Atlas.

In quoting the Bible, we intentionally used an old translation—the King James Version—and not one of the modern translations whose language is more attuned to modern times. The translation was completed at the beginning of the seventeenth century, in the days of William Shakespeare, by a group of scholars from among his circle. Its archaic language is in harmony with the Hebrew Bible both in its majesty and in its simplicity. There is no other translation that preserves the flavor of the Hebrew Bible better than this one. Of the King James Version, one is tempted to speculate that had the Bible originally been in English, this is the way it would have been written.

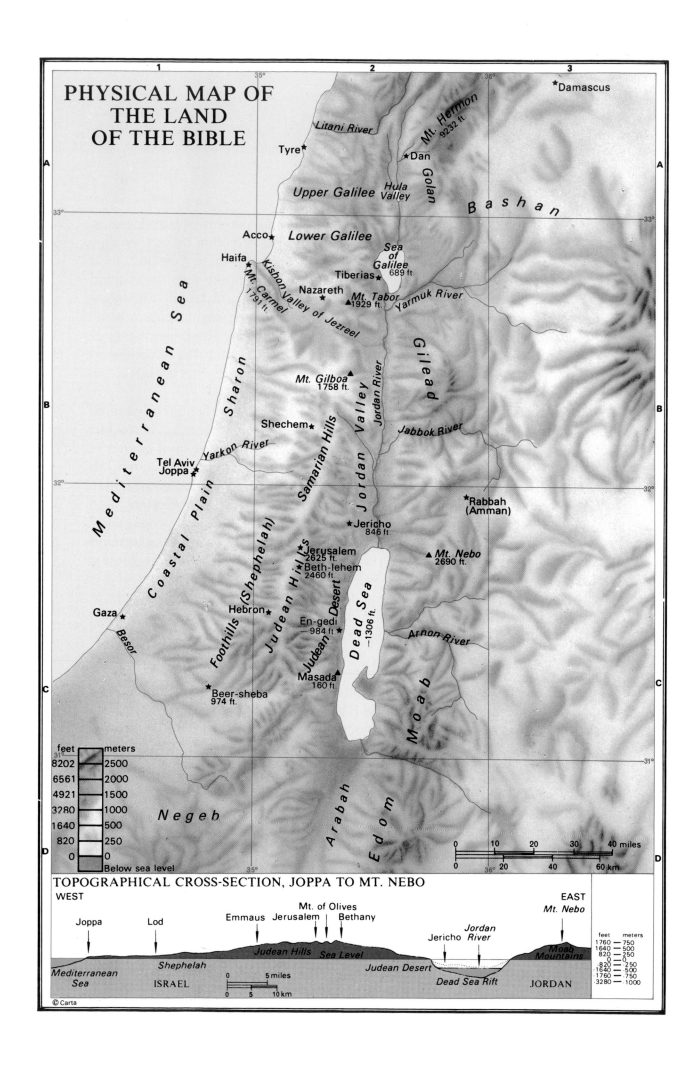

PHYSICAL MAP OF THE LAND OF THE BIBLE

★Damascus

Litani River

Mt. Hermon
9232 ft.

Tyre★

★Dan

Golan

Upper Galilee   Hula Valley

Bashan

Acco★   Lower Galilee

Haifa★   Sea of Galilee
689 ft.

Mt. Carmel   Kishon   Tiberias★
1791 ft.   Valley   Nazareth
of Jezreel   ★   Mt. Tabor
▲1929 ft.   Yarmuk River

Mediterranean Sea

Sharon

Mt. Gilboa ▲
1758 ft.

Gilead

Jordan River

Shechem★

Jordan Valley

Jabbok River

Yarkon River

Tel Aviv
Joppa★★

Coastal Plain

★Rabbah
(Amman)

★Jericho
846 ft.

Jerusalem★
2625 ft.

Judean Hills

Foothills (Shephelah)

★ Beth-lehem
2460 ft.

▲ Mt. Nebo
2690 ft.

Gaza★

Hebron★

En-gedi
984 ft.★

Judean Desert

Dead Sea
-1306 ft.

Besor

Masada ▲
160 ft.

Arnon River

Moab

Beer-sheba★
974 ft.

feet   meters
8202   2500
6561   2000
4921   1500
3280   1000
1640   500
820   250
0   0
            Below sea level

Negeb

Arabah

Edom

10   20   30   40 miles
0   20   40   60 km

TOPOGRAPHICAL CROSS-SECTION, JOPPA TO MT. NEBO

WEST   EAST
Mt. Nebo

Joppa   Lod   Emmaus   Mt. of Olives   Jericho   Jordan River
Jerusalem   Bethany

feet   meters
1760   750
1640   500
820   250
0   0
-820   -250
-1640   -500
-1760   -750
-3280   -1000

Mediterranean Sea   Shephelah   Judean Hills   Sea Level
ISRAEL   Judean Desert   Moab Mountains
Dead Sea Rift   JORDAN

0   5 miles
0   5   10 km

© Carta

8

The Hebrew Bible

The Hebrew word for Bible, *Tanakh*, is an acronym of the words *Torah* (The Five Books of Moses or Pentateuch), *Nevi'im* (The Prophets), and *Ketuvim* (The Writings or Hagiographa). These three sections of the Bible are referred to as sacred texts or sacred writings in order to distinguish them from contemporary noncanonical works known as the Apocrypha. The Bible is also known in English as Scriptures, a term more or less parallel to the Hebrew *Mikra*, which means "reading," and refers to the fact that the biblical texts were written (not oral) and, therefore, read. The term *Mikra* serves also to distinguish the books of the Bible from the Mishnah and Midrash, which originally were not committed to writing. The Bible is divided into 24 books (see below).

The selection of the books and their inclusion among the sacred writings began in the Second Temple period. The books that were not included, or were stored, were either lost or remained as part of the Apocrypha. The division into chapters and verses began in talmudic times, and developed gradually until it was finalized in the ninth century, with the addition of cantillation signs (*ta'amei ha-mikra*), which indicate the emphasized syllable of each word and the proper musical intonation as well as serving as a kind of punctuation mark. In the tenth century, the sages of Tiberias completed the work of the Masorah, i.e., the reading of each word of the Bible together with its vocalization (*nikkud*). The present division into chapters was established by Christian scholars in the Middle Ages. Jews adapted this division in the fourteenth century and it became widely known after the first Hebrew Bible was printed in Venice in the sixteenth century (apparently in order to facilitate the Jewish-Christian disputations of the time). In the Middle Ages the Pentateuch was also divided into the portions read weekly in the synagogue. This reading is done solely from a Torah scroll, a copy of the Pentateuch handwritten on parchment. Those qualified to produce such a Torah scroll are known as scribes (in Hebrew, *sofer stam*).

As the rank and file of the Jewish people became less knowledgeable of Hebrew, the need for translations of the Bible arose. Among the earliest and best known of these is the Greek translation known as the Septuagint, which was completed during the Second Temple period. There also exist a number of ancient translations into Aramaic, which was the spoken language of the Jews. Best known among these are *Targum Onkelos*, *Targum Jonathan*, and *Targum Yerushalmi* (Palestinian Targum). The Bible was later translated into Latin (the Vulgate) and, eventually, into almost every language in the world, with new and revised translations of the Bible being published all the time.

The Bible is the basis of all Jewish culture. The Mishnah (secondary work) and Talmud are based directly on the Pentateuch, and the entire Bible served as material for the *midrashim* (works of biblical exposition and homiletics that originated in the Second Temple period and continued to be produced until the twelfth century). Central to the Bible is the belief in the One God, who created the world and chose the people of Israel to be His model nation. The books of the Bible can be classified according to content: the Pentateuch—the story of the covenant the Lord made with the children of Israel; the Former Prophets—the realization of this covenant (by fulfilling God's commandments on the part of the people, and by settling the land of Israel on the part of God) and its fruition; the Latter Prophets—God's punishment of the nation for not obeying His orders and His guiding them toward salvation through prophecy; the Hagiographa—addressing God in prayer, individually or as a nation (Psalms), Wisdom Literature (Proverbs, Job, Ecclesiastes), memorial volumes (Daniel, Ezra and Nehemiah), the history of Israel (Chronicles), and the books known as the Five Scrolls. The books of the Bible were written in different forms, both structurally and linguistically: in narrative form, by historical account, verse or proverb, laws and statutes, parables, rebuke, and prayer. The means of interpreting the Bible are also varied, e.g., by means of plain, literal interpretation, fables, allegory, biblical criticism, literary analysis, and more.

The teaching of the Bible plays a central role in Western religious education, and is important in secular education as well. The Bible has been and continues to be used as a source of inspiration for religious, social and national movements, as well as for all types of art, especially literature. The Bible has immense influence on the three great monotheistic religions—Judaism, Christianity, and Islam and all the cultures associated with them. To this day the Bible is one of the most popular, revered, and most quoted books in the world.

TORAH (Pentateuch, The Five Books of Moses)		(The Latter Prophets)		KETUVIM (The Writings, Hagiographa)	
1	Genesis בְּרֵאשִׁית	10	Isaiah יְשַׁעְיָהוּ	14	Psalms תְּהִלִּים
2	Exodus שְׁמוֹת	11	Jeremiah יִרְמְיָהוּ	15	Proverbs מִשְׁלֵי
3	Leviticus וַיִּקְרָא	12	Ezekiel יְחֶזְקֵאל	16	Job אִיּוֹב
4	Numbers בְּמִדְבַּר	13	**The 12 Minor Prophets:**			
5	Deuteronomy דְּבָרִים		Hosea הוֹשֵׁעַ		**The Five Scrolls:**
			Joel יוֹאֵל	17	The Song of Songs שִׁיר הַשִּׁירִים
NEVI'IM (The Former Prophets)			Amos עָמוֹס		
			Obadiah עֹבַדְיָה	18	Ruth רוּת
6	Joshua יְהוֹשֻׁעַ		Jonah יוֹנָה	19	Lamentations אֵיכָה
7	Judges שׁוֹפְטִים		Micah מִיכָה	20	Ecclesiastes קֹהֶלֶת
8	Samuel שְׁמוּאֵל		Nahum נַחוּם	21	Esther אֶסְתֵּר
9	Kings מְלָכִים		Habakkuk חֲבַקּוּק		
			Zephaniah צְפַנְיָה	22	Daniel דָּנִיֵּאל
			Haggai חַגַּי	23	Ezra, Nehemiah עֶזְרָא-נְחֶמְיָה
			Zechariah זְכַרְיָה		
			Malachi מַלְאָכִי	24	Chronicles דִּבְרֵי הַיָּמִים

The Books of the Bible

Pentateuch (The Five Books of Moses)

Genesis (*Bereishit* in Hebrew) opens with the verse: "In the beginning (*Bereishit*) God created the heaven and earth," whence the book's name. It has 50 chapters. The first eleven recount the story of the Creation up to the building of the Tower of Babel. The remaining chapters give an account of the lives of the Patriarchs until the descent into Egypt.

Exodus (in Hebrew, *Shemot*) opens with the verse: "Now these are the names (*shemot*) of the children of Israel, which came into Egypt." Its 40 chapters give an account of the enslavement in Egypt, the Exodus from Egypt, the Song at the Sea, the first wanderings of the Israelites in the wilderness, the Giving of the Law on Mount Sinai—the Ten Commandments, the building of the Sanctuary and its utensils and the priestly duties within the Sanctuary.

Leviticus (in Hebrew, *Vayikra*) opens with "And the Lord called (*Vayikra*) unto Moses. . . ." The book's 27 chapters deal mostly with the Temple service and holy matters: sacrificial laws; the consecration of Aaron and his sons; laws concerning forbidden food, ritual uncleanliness and purity; the order of worship on Yom Kippur; laws of incest; consecration of the priests; laws concerning the Sabbath and festivals, vows and dedications, the Sabbatical and Jubilee years, and reward and punishment. The book is also known as the "Priest's Manual."

Numbers (in Hebrew, *Bemidbar*) begins with the verse: "And the Lord spake unto Moses in the wilderness (*bemidbar*) of Sinai. . . ." It has 36 chapters, about a third of which continues with the historical record of Israel in the wilderness after the Exodus; the rest deals with the laws of the sacrifices and religious worship in the Temple. It is also referred to as the "*Hummash* (i.e., Pentateuchal volume) of the Numbered," for both at the beginning and toward the end of the book there is a census of the Israelites.

Deuteronomy (in Hebrew, *Devarim*) opens with "These be the words (*devarim*) which Moses spake. . . ." It has 34 chapters. It is also referred to as *Mishneh Torah* (i.e., "the Repetition of the Torah," whence the Greek *Deuteronomion*—"Second Law"), because it repeats much of the laws previously recorded in the Pentateuch. It contains a survey of the Jews until their arrival at the plains of Moab, various laws and statutes, the blessing in reward for observing the Torah and the punishment for disobeying it, the account of Moses' final acts, his parting benediction to the tribes and his death.

The Former Prophets

Joshua gives an account of the acts and wars of Joshua, son of Nun, leader of the Israelites after the death of Moses. The book's 24 chapters deal with the conquest of the land of Canaan (chs. 1–12), the division of the land among the tribes and the establishment of the cities of refuge (chs. 13–22), and Joshua's final will and testament and his death (chs. 23–24).

Judges chronicles the period between the conquest of the land of Canaan and the establishment of the monarchy. During this time, leaders of the tribes, who were called Judges, occasionally rose to power, usually in times of danger, to defend their tribe or several nearby tribes against the enemy; after their successes the Judges would remain leaders also in times of peace, and some became leaders without any threat of war. The book contains 21 chapters.

Samuel is named after the last Judge and the only one who was leader of all the tribes of Israel. After the translation of the Septuagint and Vulgate editions, the book, because of its length, was divided in two: *I Samuel*, with 31 chapters, and *II Samuel* with 24. Based on the central figures there are three parts: the story of Samuel (I Sam. 1–12); Saul and his dynasty, until his death and burial (I Sam. 13–II Sam. 1); and the story of David's rule (II Sam. 2–24).

Kings is divided in two parts, *I Kings* (22 chapters) and *II Kings* (25 chapters). This division came relatively late and does not reflect the thematic contents of the book. The Book of Kings describes the last days of King David, the kingdom of Solomon, the split of the United Monarchy, the histories of the kingdoms of Judah and Israel (including lists of all the kings and the dates of their reign), the exile of the Ten Tribes, the end of the kingdom of Judah, and the Babylonian exile.

The Latter Prophets

Isaiah is, according to tradition, the prophecies of one prophet, Isaiah, son of Amoz. Most modern Bible scholars, however, suggest that while the first 39 chapters of the book are the work of Isaiah, who prophesied in the second half of the eighth century BCE, chapters 40 to 66 were written by another, anonymous prophet, who was active in the beginning of the seventh century BCE. Because both parts are arranged in one book, the second author has been named the second Isaiah (Deutero-Isaiah). According to its contents the book is divided into three parts. Chapters 1 to 35 include prophecies of calamitous suffering, future redemption, wrath and rebuke, and the end of days; chapters 36 to 39 describe events that occurred during the reign of King Hezekiah; and chapters 40 to 66 relate prophecies of redemption, as well as the end of days and Judgment Day.

Jeremiah is the book of the prophet Jeremiah, son of Hilkiah, who prophesied in Judah for about 40 years, from the reign of Josiah to the destruction of the First Temple. There are 52 chapters: chapters 1 to 25 relate prophecies of wrath and rebuke; chapters 26 to 45, various prophecies interspersed with biographical details; chapters 46 to 51, oracles against foreign nations; and the last chapter, 52, describes the final days of the kingdom of Judah and the history of King Jehoiachin in Babylon.

Ezekiel is the book of the prophet Ezekiel, son of Buzi the priest, who lived in the time of the destruction of the First Temple, and who was exiled to Babylon with King Jehoiachin (in 597 BCE), settling in Tel-abib, by the river Chebar. The book has 48 chapters. Chapters 1 to 24 tell of the call of the prophet and the prophecies of doom and destruction of Jerusalem; chapters 25 to 32 relate oracles of doom against foreign nations; chapters 33 to 39, prophecies of consolation and of Israel's restoration; and chapters 40 to 48 describe the complete restoration, plans for the future Temple, the laws of the priests, and the division of the land among the tribes of Israel.

The Twelve Minor Prophets

Hosea is the book of the prophet Hosea, son of Beeri, who prophesied in the days of Uzziah, Jotham, Ahaz, and Hezekiah, kings of Judah, and in the days of Jeroboam, son of Joash, king of Israel. His prophecies were mostly addressed to the northern kingdom of Israel. The book has 14 chapters, the first part of which (chs. 1–3) includes prophecies interspersed with biographical events. Chapters 4 to 14 contain prophecies of the crimes of Israel, their forewarned punishment, and of the coming redemption.

Joel is the book of the prophet Joel, son of Pethuel. The time of his prophecies was already disputed in the mishnaic and talmudic periods. Some maintain that Joel prophesied in the days of Jehoram, son of Ahab, while others suggest that he was active in the days of Manasseh. Modern scholars place him later, up to the time of the Return to Zion (late sixth – early fifth centuries BCE). The book has four chapters. The first two describe a plague of locusts and a call for repentance; the last two warn of punishment against the nations who have wronged the Jews and a promise of the return to Zion.

Amos is the book of the prophet Amos, a shepherd of Tekoa, who prophesied in the days of King Uzziah of Judah and in the days of Jeroboam, son of Joash, king of Israel. He was a contemporary of Hosea, Isaiah, and Micah. In the book's nine chapters, Amos demands justice and righteousness, fights against social injustice, and reproves the wealthy classes for pursuing their own pleasure while oppressing the poor, the people at large for worshiping idols, and those who would seek the help of foreign nations.

Obadiah is the book of the prophet Obadiah who, according to modern scholars, was active after the destruction of the First Temple. The book consists of one chapter with 21 verses. It prophesies that Edom would be destroyed as a result of its pride and hatred for Israel, and would be plundered by its enemies.

Jonah describes the mission of Jonah, son of Amittai, to Nineveh and all that he incurred. Jonah probably prophesied in the days of Jeroboam II, king of Israel. The book's four chapters describe the power of repentance and the greatness of God's mercy.

Micah is the book of the prophet Micah the Morasthite. He prophesied in the days of Jotham, Ahaz, and Hezekiah, kings of Judah, and was a contemporary of the prophets Amos, Hosea, and Isaiah. The book has seven chapters, dealing with the prophet's rebuke of corruption and oppression that will lead to destruction, and a prophecy of salvation that will bring a new and better world, based on universal brotherhood and peace.

Nahum is the book of the prophet Nahum the Elkoshite, who prophesied in Judah from the middle of King Manasseh's reign to the end of Josiah's rule. The book contains three chapters, which mainly envision the destruction of Nineveh.

Habakkuk is the book of the prophet Habakkuk. According to one tradition, the prophet lived in the time of Manasseh, king of Judah. Modern scholars, however, place him in the time of Jehoiakim; others suggest he prophesied after the destruction of the First Temple. The book has three chapters; the first two include a complaint about the evil that rules the world, a description of the victory of the Chaldeans, and their downfall. Chapter 3 is a psalm that describes the appearance of God bringing salvation to His people.

Zephaniah is the book of the prophet Zephaniah, son of Cushi, who prophesied in the days of Josiah. His prophecies were aimed at strengthening Josiah's religious and social reforms. The book has three chapters, dealing with the denunciation of idolatry in Judah, the Day of Judgment and Divine punishment, a prophecy concerning the neighboring nations, and the days of God's mercy after His anger subsides.

Haggai is the book of the prophet Haggai, in the days of the Return to Zion. The book's two chapters call for the completion of the Temple, compassion for the people, and the demand to keep the Temple sanctified; the book also prophesies the fall of the heathen kingdoms and God's choice of Zerubbabel, son of Shealtiel, to be His messenger.

Zechariah is the book of the prophet Zechariah, son of Berechiah, in the days of the Return to Zion. The book has 14 chapters. Chapters 1 to 8 contain visions of the building of Jerusalem, the nation's leaders, the purification of the land, the judgment of the world, and the beginning of the messianic era. Chapters 9 to 14 relate prophecies of the final days of Ephraim, Judah and several neighboring nations; these chapters are considered by some scholars to be the words of a different prophet (the "second Zechariah"), or even of two other prophets, who lived in the time of Antiochus' decrees and the Hasmonean revolt, or who lived much earlier, in the time of the First Temple.

Malachi is the book of the last prophet, Malachi, who lived in the days of Ezra and Nehemiah. The book's three chapters deal mainly with the prophet's fight against such negative phenomena as mixed marriages, nonpayment of tithes to the Temple, and oppression, in order to save the people from the danger of annihilation.

The Hagiographa

Psalms is a collection of 150 poems, most of which are hymns to God. The book is divided into five parts (chs. 1–41; 42–72; 73–89; 90–106; and 107–150). According to tradition, the authorship is ascribed to King David. Modern scholars suggest that some psalms were written before David, some were written in the time of David, and still others during the Babylonian exile. The psalms consist mainly of hymns of praise, elegies, but also wonderment and complaints. Many psalms were incorporated in the Jewish prayer book; Christian liturgy also makes extensive use of the psalms.

Proverbs belongs to the genre of Wisdom Literature and is attributed to King Solomon, "the wisest of all men." Some proverbs are ascribed to other sages. The proverbs appeal to man as a universal being, and not to the Israel nation in particular. Its 31 chapters deal with state and social matters, friendship and family relations, joy and sadness, commerce, trade, and other topics.

Job has as its central theme the issue of reward and punishment and, principally, the question of why "the righteous suffer while the wicked thrive." This book, like Proverbs, does not indicate a special relation to the nation of Israel. According to the book's content and structure, it is categorized as Wisdom Literature. The book contains 42 chapters. The date of its composition is generally ascribed to the Second Temple period (fifth–fourth centuries BCE).

The Five Scrolls

The Song of Songs is a collection of love poems between bride and groom. The book has eight chapters. Jewish tradition ascribes its composition to King Solomon and views the book as an allegorical description of the love between God and the nation of Israel. The Song of Songs is read during Passover.

Ruth recounts the story of Ruth the Moabitess, a model convert to Judaism from whom King David was descended. The book has four chapters and its story illustrates a number of Jewish laws: e.g., donations to the poor; *halitzah* (i.e., the act of "releasing" a childless widow for remarriage by the brother-in-law); and redemption of the lands. The story occurs during the harvest season and is thus read in the synagogue during the festival of Shavuot (Pentecost).

Lamentations (in Hebrew, *Ekhah*) derives its name from the first word in the opening verse ("How doth [*Ekhah*] . . ."). The author, traditionally ascribed to Jeremiah, laments the destruction of the First Temple. The book has five chapters, each with 22 verses (ch. 3 has 66 verses—22 × 3), the opening letters of which are arranged in Hebrew alphabetical order. Lamentations is read on the eve of the Ninth of Av, the fast day that commemorates the destruction of the Temple, and is reread during that day.

Ecclesiastes, like Proverbs and Job, belongs to the genre of Wisdom Literature. According to tradition, it was written by King Solomon in his old age. Bible scholars, however, date its composition to the Second Temple period. The book has 12 chapters. It is read in the synagogue during Sukkot (Feast of Tabernacles).

Esther recounts how the Jews of Persia and Media were saved from destruction in the days of King Ahasuerus (early fifth century BCE). This salvation is credited to Esther, who was married to Ahasuerus. To commemorate the event, the feast of Purim was established on the 14th and 15th of the Hebrew month of Adar, when the Book of Esther (ten chapters) is read in the synagogue twice, at both the evening and morning services.

Daniel tells the story of Daniel and his companions in the royal courts of Nebuchadnezzar, Darius, and Belshazzar, and the visions of Daniel concerning four symbolic kingdoms (referring to Babylon, Media, Persia, and Greece), which would be succeeded by a kingdom of heaven. Some of the book's 12 chapters are written in Hebrew (1:1–2:4; 8–12), the remainder in Aramaic (2:4–7:28). The time and place of its composition are unclear; according to some scholars, it was written in the time of Antiochus' decrees, in 167 BCE. Because the book deals with the end of days, it became a cornerstone in the development of Jewish mysticism, of the messianic concept, and the belief in the resurrection of the dead.

Ezra tells of the Return to Zion. The book has ten chapters: the first six describe the early stages of the return, from Cyrus' decree in 538 BCE to the dedication of the Temple in 515 BCE, in the time of Darius I; chapters 7 to 10 tell of Ezra's own return to the Holy Land, in the days of Artaxerxes until the banishing of the foreign wives (458–426 BCE). The books of Ezra and Nehemiah were originally a single book called Ezra, and only in the mid-fifteenth century were they divided in two; nevertheless, in Jewish tradition they are still considered a single work.

Nehemiah tells the story of Nehemiah, son of Hachaliah, who was appointed governor of Judah (444–437 BCE) by the Persian ruler, Artaxerxes I. The book has 13 chapters. Under Nehemiah's leadership, Judah was restored, the Jewish community was strengthened, the walls of Jerusalem were repaired, the number of inhabitants increased, the situation of the poor improved, the tax burden was eased, the Temple service was reinstituted, Sabbath observance intensified, and mixed marriages were banned.

Chronicles is, according to Jewish tradition, the last book of the Bible. The book is divided in two—*I Chronicles* (29 chapters) and *II Chronicles* (31 chapters)—in accordance with the Septuagint edition. Opinions differ as to the date of composition: according to some scholars, it was written in the fourth century BCE, together with the Book of Ezra. The book chronicles the history of the kings of Judah and their genealogies. Some discrepancies are found between Chronicles and the Former Prophets.

Aramaic translation, 5th century BCE, of Behistun Inscription of Darius I, recounting his many city conquests.

The Ancient Near East

The land to which Abraham came and to which Moses brought the Israelites after their Exodus from Egypt—the land of Canaan, namely, the land of Israel—is bound by the Great Sea, i.e., the Mediterranean Sea on the west, by hills and high mountains on the north and northeast, and by deserts on the east and south.

Physically, the land of Israel forms part of a block of lands that extend in a crescent-like shape from the Persian Gulf in the east, to Mesopotamia (Aram-naharaim) in the north, and to the Sinai peninsula in the west—the so-called Fertile Crescent. Its fertility stems from the great rivers of the Tigris and Euphrates that pass through the Mesopotamian lands, and the broad plains extending between and alongside those rivers and their tributaries. The land of Israel is less fortunate, for it is at the narrow and lean southwestern edge of the Fertile Crescent, with fewer and much shorter rivers and narrower and less fertile plains.

Another land of large rivers—Egypt, also nicknamed the "land of the Nile"—lies to the south of the land of Israel.

Great rivers supply water for sustenance and irrigation and serve as convenient arteries of communication, thus providing a nucleus and natural base for the development of organized, consolidated and regimented civilizations. Such civilizations arose already in the fourth millennium: the kingdoms of Sumer and Accad, Mitanni and Heth, Babylonia and Assyria, and Media and Persia, established on the banks of the Euphrates and the Tigris; and the kingdom of Egypt, along the Nile, which, because of its location, was more confined and homogeneous for development.

The geopolitical position of the land of Israel between these two civilizations—Mesopotamia and Egypt—determined its historical fate as a land-bridge and international crossroad, and often as an arena for battles between competing powers.

The general survey presented here describes the changes that the Middle East underwent in the second and first millennia, changes which are interwoven with the biblical period, from the time of the Patriarchs to the Return to Zion.

In the beginning of the second millennium, in the Euphrates and Tigris valley, there arose the Babylonian kingdom, which would subsequently know intermittent periods of expansion and secession. The Mari kingdom, in the middle Euphrates region, expanded its rule westward in the eighteenth century BCE, followed by the Mitanni kingdom, which grew and flourished in the area of the upper Euphrates.

In the second millennium, the Egyptian kingdom enjoyed two periods of power and expansion—that of the Middle Kingdom (12th Dynasty) in c. 1991–1786 BCE, and the New Kingdom (18th–20th Dynasties) in c. 1570–1150 BCE. Between these two periods, the Hyksos, a Semitic tribe, reigned over the land of Israel and extended their rule up to the Euphrates.

After the expulsion of the Hyksos, the Pharaohs of Egypt sought to expand their rule into the land of Israel and Syria. Egypt's rivals

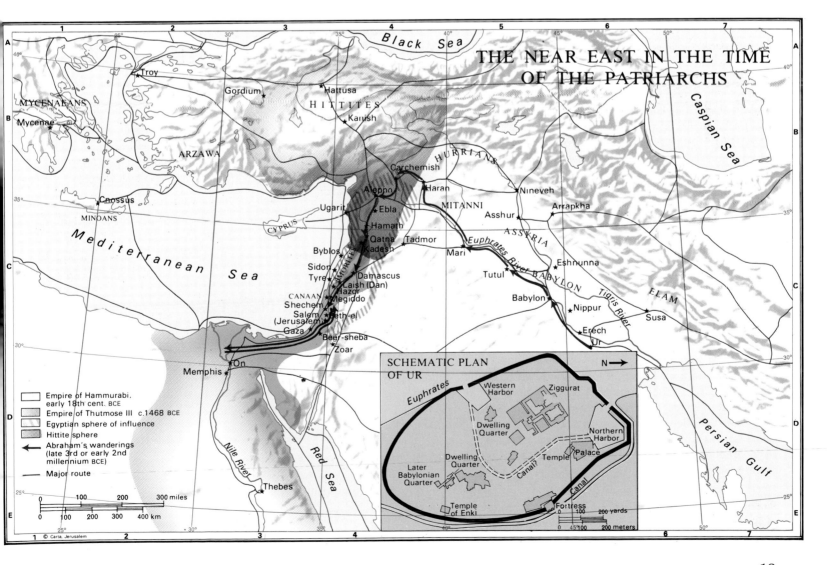

THE NEAR EAST IN THE TIME OF THE PATRIARCHS

Empire of Hammurabi, early 18th cent. BCE
Empire of Thutmose III c.1468 BCE
Egyptian sphere of influence
Hittite sphere
Abraham's wanderings (late 3rd or early 2nd millennium BCE)
Major route

SCHEMATIC PLAN OF UR

in the north were the Mitanni kingdom and, later, the Hittite kingdom, established in Asia Minor in c. 1800 BCE, which grew in power and expanded its rule to Syria, reaching its peak in the days of King Shuppiluliuma (c. 1380–1350 BCE). For stability and to prevent unrest, the Pharaohs occasionally set out on military campaigns. The best known of these were the campaigns of Thutmose III and the battle of Megiddo (fifteenth century BCE), the campaigns of Amenhotep (1431; 1429), Seti I (1303), Rameses II and the battle of Kedesh (1286), and the campaign of Merneptah (1220). Following the battle of Kedesh, a treaty was signed between Egypt and the Hittites, a treaty that was reinforced by the marriage of Rameses II to a Hittite princess. The Hittite kingdom collapsed in 1200 BCE, and Egypt again suffered a period of recession toward the end of the second millennium.

The period of the Patriarchs, as told in the books of Genesis and Exodus, began in about the middle of the second millennium. According to the biblical narrative, Abraham left Ur of the Chaldees, in southern Mesopotamia, and settled for awhile in Haran, east of the upper Euphrates. From there he wandered into the land of Canaan, where there was an abundance of city-states. The Patriarchs led their lives as nomadic shepherds. Once, because of drought and famine, Abraham descended into Egypt. His descendants kept ties with Haran but with the continuing drought, many of them also descended into Egypt, remaining there for four generations. The Exodus from Egypt, under the leadership of Moses, and the period of settlement in Canaan, under Joshua, mark the beginning of the history of the Israelites as a nation. The settlement of the land was an ongoing process, thought to have begun prior to the 13th century BCE and ending thereafter. Egyptian sources mention the name "Israel" on the Merneptah Stele (thus also called the Israel Stele) from 1220 BCE—testimony to the Israelites' existence in Canaan during that period.

During the period of conquest and settlement, the powers lying to the south and west of the land of Israel were in an extremely weakened state, leaving the Israelites to contend only with the city-states of Canaan and with the Sea Peoples, whose penetration reached its height at the beginning of the twelfth century BCE. In the beginning of the first millennium, the kings of Egypt once again sought to renew Egyptian rule in Canaan. In the days of King Rehoboam, the Egyptian king Shishak captured Jerusalem (in 924 BCE) and plundered the treasures of the Temple and the king's palace; still, he failed to establish his rule over the area he had conquered.

Between 1000 and 612 BCE, Assyria was the ruling power in the Middle East. In the battle of Qarqar in 853, the western kings attempted to form an alliance, headed by Hadad-ezer of Damascus, Ahab of Israel, and Irhuleni of Hamath, in order to halt the Assyrian army. However, after a few years, the Assyrians returned and proved invincible. One kingdom fell after the other: Damascus in 732, Israel (Samaria) in 722, and Judah became a subject-nation. At its height, Assyria's power spread over Elam, southeast Asia Minor, Syria, the land of the Philistines and, for a period, Upper Egypt, with its capital No-Amon (Thebes) plundered in 663 BCE.

Assyrian rule eventually fell to the Medes, in the east, and the Babylonians, in the south, who divided the former Assyrian territory among themselves. The capital of Nineveh was destroyed by the Medes in 612 BCE. The Babylonian kingdom reached its greatest extent in the days of Nebuchadnezzar II, who defeated the king of Egypt in the battle of Carchemish, in 605, and who brought an end to Assyrian rule in Elam, northern Syria, and in Asia Minor. In 598, Nebuchadnezzar ascended upon Jerusalem to suppress the rebellion led by Jehoiakim, king of Judah. He again returned to Judah, following Zedekiah's rebellion, at which time he destroyed one Judean city after another, burned Jerusalem and the Temple, and banished many of its inhabitants. Another exile occurred in 582 BCE, perhaps as a result of a further revolt.

The Median kingdom remained in power until 550 BCE, when it fell into the hands of the Persian king Cyrus, who annexed it to his kingdom. Within a few years, Cyrus succeeded in spreading his kingdom westward, to the Aegean Sea, and in 539 he captured Babylon. Cyrus, or "Cyrus the Great," is mentioned in the Bible thanks to his declaration allowing the exiled Jews of Babylon to return to their land. The land of Israel became a Persian province. Among its appointed governors were Zerubbabel, son of Shealtiel, and Nehemiah, son of Hachaliah, during whose time the Return to Zion had begun, the walls of Jerusalem were repaired, and the Temple was rebuilt. The Persian Empire, which remained in power for 200 years, extended from India to Cush (Nubia),

The Peoples and Lands of the Ancient Near East

Canaan is the ancient name of the land of Israel. It was promised to Abraham and his descendants, and was the land to which Abraham came from Haran. It was conquered by Joshua. Before and at the time of the conquest, Canaan was inhabited by seven nations: the Hittites, Perizzites, Amorites, Canaanites, Girgashites, Hivites, and the Jebusites. In some instances in the Bible, the name refers only to a Mediterranean coastal strip; in others, it refers to a large area that included Transjordan, southern Syria, and the eastern Sinai.

Amorites were a Semitic nation who settled in Syria and the land of Israel. At the end of the third millennium and the beginning of the second, they invaded Mesopotamia, captured Babylon, in whose culture they assimilated, and developed several small kingdoms. Many of the Babylonian kings were Amorites, among them Hammurabi (1792–1750 BCE), known for his famous law code. According to the Bible, they were mountain dwellers, contrary to the Canaanites, who settled in the valleys and on the coastal plain.

Hittites were an Indo-European-speaking nation who appeared in Anatolia and established the ancient kingdom of Heth (1700–1230 BCE), which, at its height, embraced most of the territory of Anatolia and Syria. Their capital was Hattusa, identified with Bogazköy. Like the Egyptians, they believed their king was an emissary of God and would turn into one at death. Their social structure was feudalistic and included slavery. Their language, though extinct, is known from hieroglyphic texts on documents and monuments, preserved for millennia in the royal archives at Hattusa. After the destruction of their kingdom, neo-Hittite kingdoms sprang up in Syria and southern Anatolia.

Edom is one of the neighboring nations of ancient Israel and close to it in origin. During the period of settlement and First Temple times, the Edomites dwelled on Mount Seir, south of the Dead Sea, but after the Babylonian exile, the desert tribes were driven away, moving to the Negeb and the Hebron hills. At the end of the First Temple period, the Edomites invaded Judah and speeded its destruction. They and their converts finally succumbed to John Hyrcanus the Hasmonean. Herod the Great was also an Edomite.

Moab was, according to the biblical narrative, the son of Lot by his eldest daughter, and chieftain of the Moabites, a Semitic nation, one of Israel's neighbors and foes who settled east of the Dead Sea. They had a highly developed culture. In the ninth century BCE, they rebelled against the Israelite conquest. The Mesha Stele, which was discovered at Dibon and dated to the ninth century BCE, bears a Moabite inscription that attests to the affinity of the Moabite script and language to those of Hebrew.

Ammonites were descendants of Ben-Ammi, the son of Lot by his youngest daughter. They lived in Transjordan, in the area of Rabbath-bene-ammon. Ammon was conquered by the tribes of Israel. The Ammonites attempted to rebel from time to time, but they were always defeated. Little evidence has been found about their culture. The few inscriptions that did survive revealed their language and script, like Moabite, are similar to Hebrew.

Amalek was a descendant of Esau, and chieftain of Edom. The ancient Amalekite nation apparently dwelled in the south and fought vigorously against the southern tribes of Israel. The Pentateuch throughout tried to eradicate the memory of this nation, and King Saul lost his throne because of his failure to do precisely that. They were finally destroyed in the days of King Hezekiah.

Assyria, an ancient kingdom in the upper Tigris valley, was named after its chief god, Asshur. The Assyrians, a Semitic nation, arrived in the Tigris valley in the middle of the third millennium, when, at first, they were a Babylonian protectorate. In the middle of the second millennium, Assyria became an empire, which was expanded in the days of Tiglath-pileser I (1120–1074 BCE), who captured the city of Babylon. In the days of Shalmaneser III (858–824), the land of Israel and Syria were also conquered. The Assyrian Empire reached its peak in the days of Tiglath-pileser III (754–725). Kings Sargon II, Sennacherib, and Esarhaddon were able to keep their domains intact, but in 612, the Babylonians and Medes captured the Assyrian capital of Nineveh and, in 609 BCE, Assyrian rule was put to an end.

Babylon is an ancient city and kingdom in the lower Euphrates valley. In the Bible, it also appears as Shinar, Chaldea, and Sheshach. The first known human culture—Sumer—developed in this area in the seventh millennium. The Babylonians were a Semitic people. The city of Babylon flourished between 2150 and 1740 BCE, in the days of the monarchical dynasty, among whose kings was Hammurabi. Afterward, it was under the threat of neighboring Assyria. The city was destroyed by the Assyrian king Sennacherib in 689, was rebuilt by Nebuchadnezzar II in 625, and was surrendered to King Cyrus the Great of Persia in 539. The kings of the new kingdom were Chaldeans, an Aramean tribe. Babylon played a significant role in the history of Israel: according to the Bible, Abraham came to Canaan from Ur of the Chaldees, Nebuchadnezzar conquered the kingdom of Judah (in 601) and exiled its people to Babylon (in 587), and, at the time of the Return to Zion by Ezra and Nehemiah, most of the people of Judah remained in Babylon.

Medes was one of the races descended from Japhet. The region southwest of the Caspian Sea was the site of the ancient kingdom of Media, whose inhabitants were seminomads. From the eighth to sixth centuries BCE, they united against Assyria and in 612, in the days of Cyaxares, they destroyed Nineveh with the help of the Babylonians. In 550, Media and Persia were combined in the expanding empire of Cyrus the Great, king of Persia.

Persia was an ancient kingdom between the Caspian Sea and the Persian Gulf. It became a large empire in the days of Cyrus the Great, in the mid-sixth century BCE. Cyrus allowed the exiled Jews to return to Judah (Zion) and to rebuild the Temple. The Book of Esther describes the events that occurred in the days of Ahasuerus (Xerxes); it is not clear, however, which Ahasuerus.

Midian was a son of Abraham and his wife Keturah, and progenitor of the Midianites, who dwelled south of the land of Canaan, between the Sinai and Edom mountains. Their origin is unknown. They wandered from the Arabian peninsula along two routes: the southern group settled on the banks of the Red Sea, in the region of Edom and south of it, while the others reached as far north as the Syrian desert. According to the Bible, the Midianites joined with the Moabites in preventing the Israelites from conquering their lands. Moses subdued them. The Israelites were under Midianite rule for seven years, until the judge Gideon rose up and expelled them, along with the Amalekites.

Aram is descended from Shem. It is the name for the Semitic peoples/tribes whose origins can probably be found west of the Euphrates. According to the Bible, the Arameans were related to the Patriarchs. Although they are first mentioned in the fourteenth century BCE, their presence increased only in the eleventh century BCE, when they spread out over extensive territories—from the Euphrates and Tigris valleys to southern Anatolia and from Armenia to northern Arabia. They established several kingdoms, over which their hegemony passed from one kingdom to the other. One of the most important was Aram-Damascus. Aramaic was an international language in the ancient world of the first millennium, until superseded by Greek. The Arameans adopted the Phoenician alphabet, from which the Hebrew square script and the Arabic script developed.

Philistines were a non-Semitic nation who arrived in Canaan in the beginning of the twelfth century BCE, repelled the attacks of the Israelites, and took control of the coastal area that was named after them—Philistia. Tradition has it that they were one of the Sea Peoples who left Crete. They were known as seafarers and for their belligerency. They remained in their kingdoms until their assimilation during the Hellenistic period.

Sea Peoples were seafaring tribes. In the thirteenth and twelfth centuries BCE, they wiped out the Hittite kingdom and settled in Asia Minor, the Aegean area, and North Africa. In 1170 BCE, they were almost completely destroyed by Rameses III, the king of Egypt. Some scholars identify them with the Achaeans, others with the Etruscans or the Philistines.

Chronology of the Old Testament

The first section of the Bible, the Pentateuch, opens with the creation of the world and ends with the death of Moses, a span of about 2,500 years, according to Jewish traditional chronological dating. The rest of the Bible (Former Prophets, Latter Prophets, Hagiographa) is placed within a period of about 800 years, from the conquest of the land of Canaan in the thirteenth century to the Return to Zion and the rebuilding of the Temple in the mid-fifth century.

Presented here is a table of the major events and their dates, some of which are conjectured, others estimated, and still others more or less exact. It should be noted that even the "exact" dates, based on one of several conventional dating methods, may differ from other such dates by a gap of ten years or less.

All the dates referred to below, and throughout this Atlas, are before the Common Era, thus precluding the need to append BCE to the year specified.

Period of the Patriarchs	1st half of 2nd
(Abraham, Isaac and Jacob)	millennium
Exodus from Egypt	1st half of 13th century
Wanderings of the Israelites	1st half of 13th century
The Israelite Entry into Transjordan	**Mid-13th century**
The Israelite entry into Canaan	Mid-13th century
Battle of Gibeon	Mid-13th century
The rise of Judah and the southern tribes	2nd half of 13th century
Conquest of the Shephelah districts	End of 13th century
Period of the Judges	**12th–11th centuries**
The war of Deborah	Beginning of 12th century
Battle of the Waters of Merom	Beginning of 12th century
Story of the concubine in Gibeah	1st half of 12th century
The war of Ehud	12th century
The war of Gideon	12th century
The kingdom of Abimelech	12th century
The war of Jephthah	End of 12th century
The deeds of Samson	1st half of 11th century
Battle of Eben-ezer	Mid-11th century
The wanderings of the Ark of the Covenant	Mid-11th century
The leadership of Samuel	2nd half of 11th century
Saul searches for his asses	2nd half of 11th century
The kingdom of Saul	1025–1006
David's duel with Goliath	1010
The kingdoms of David and Eshbaal	1006–1004
The battle by the pool at Gibeon	1005
David's conquest of Jerusalem	1004
The Philistine wars of David	1000
The Kingdom of David	**990–968**
David's campaigns in Transjordan	990
The conquest of Aram-zobah and Damascus	990
The conquest of Edom	990
The rebellion of Absalom	978
The rebellion of Sheba the son of Bichri	977
The Kingdom of Solomon	**968–928**
Division of the Monarchy	**928**

Kingdom of Judah		Kingdom of Israel		Wars/Military Campaigns	
Rehoboam	928–911	Jeroboam	928–907	Shishak's campaign	924
Abijah	911–908			Conquests of Abijah	911
Asa	908–867	Nadab	907–906	Zerah's campaign	900
		Baasha	906–883	Wars of Asa and Baasha	855
		Elah	883–882	Ben-hadad I's campaign	
		Zimri	882	Conquests of Mesha, king of Moab	
		Omri	882–871		
		Ahab	871–851	Ahab's wars in Aram	855–850
Jehoshaphat	867–851			Battle of Qarqar	853
Jehoram	851–843	Ahaziah	851–850		
		Jehoram	850–842		
Ahaziah	843–842				
Athaliah	842–836	Jehu	842–814	Shalmaneser III's campaign	841
Joash	836–799	Jehoahaz	814–800	Hazael's campaigns	815–810
		Joash	800–785	Adad-nirari's campaign	806
				Conquests of Joash and Jeroboam II	790–770
Amaziah	799–786			Wars of Amaziah and Joash	786
Uzziah	786–758	Jeroboam II	785–749	Uzziah's conquests	Mid-8th century
Jotham	758–742	Zechariah	749		
		Shallum	748		
		Menahem	748–737		
Ahaz	742–726	Pekahiah	737–735		
		Pekah	735–731	Rezin and Pekah's campaign in Judah	734
		Exile of Israel	733		
		Hoshea	731–722		
Hezekiah	726–697	Fall of Samaria	722		
		Assyrian rule	722–628	Sennacherib's campaign	701
Manasseh	697–642				
Amon	642–640				
Josiah	640–609	Josiah's rule	628–609		
Jehoahaz	609–608	Egyptian rule	609–604	Pharaoh Necho's campaign	609
Jehoiakim	608–597	Babylonian rule	604–539	Nebuchadnezzar's campaign	605–604
Jehoiachin	597				
Zedekiah	597–587				
Exile of Judah	597				
Destruction of the First Temple	587			Nebuchadnezzar's campaign	587
Babylonian rule	587–538				
Persian rule	538 ff.	Persian rule	538 ff.		
Cyrus' decree	538				
Return to Zion	538–445				
Zerubbabel governs Judah	522				
Building of the Temple	520–515				
Ezra	457–445				
Nehemiah	445–425				

The Patriarchs

According to the Bible, Patriarch is the traditional name given to each of the three fathers of the Jewish nation: Abraham, Isaac, and Jacob. In Jewish tradition it is customary to add the Hebrew epithet *Avinu* ("Our Father") to each name. They are seen as spiritual prototypes of the nation of Israel.

Abraham (in the beginning called Abram), the son of Terah, brother of Nahor and Haran, is the first of the three Patriarchs. He left the faith of his forefathers, who were idol worshipers, for the belief in one God. He abandoned his father's house and his homeland, Ur of the Chaldees, and descended into the land of Canaan. Through him was made the covenant between the nation of Israel and God, symbolized in the Jewish circumcision ceremony. God promised him that he would be the father of a multitude of nations and that his descendants would inherit the land of Canaan. Abraham and his wife Sarah are buried in the Cave of Machpelah, in Hebron.

Isaac, the son born to Abraham and Sarah in their old age, is the second of the three Patriarchs. He was destined to be sacrificed by his father Abraham at God's command (the "binding of Isaac"). He married Rebekah, the daughter of Bethuel, sister of Laban, of his father's family. He was the only Patriarch who lived his entire life in the land of Canaan. He and Rebekah, like his parents before him, are buried in the Cave of Machpelah.

Jacob, the son of Isaac and Rebekah, is the last of the Patriarchs. He bought the birthright from his twin brother Esau "for bread and pottage of lentils" (Gen. 25:34). Jacob married Leah and Rachel, the daughters of Laban, son of Bethuel. His 12 sons were the progenitors of the tribes of Israel. In the years of drought, he descended with his sons into Egypt. He died in Goshen but his remains were brought for burial in the tomb of his forefathers, the Cave of Machpelah, where his wife Leah was buried before him (his second wife, Rachel, was buried in the way to Ephrath). Jacob was also called Israel, after which the nation, the children and the land of Israel were named.

The Matriarchs

Traditionally, Matriarch is the name given to each of the wives of the three Patriarchs: Sarah, the wife of Abraham; Rebekah, the wife of Isaac; and Leah and Rachel, the wives of Jacob. In Jewish tradition it is customary to add the Hebrew epithet *Imenu* ("Our Mother") to each name. Sarah, Rebekah and Leah were buried alongside their husbands in the Cave of Machpelah; Rachel was buried in the way to Ephrath ("Rachel's Tomb").

Sarah (in the beginning called Sarai) was the wife of Abraham and the first of the four Matriarchs. She was barren and gave her handmaid Hagar to Abraham so that he would be granted offspring, but when Hagar gave birth to Ishmael, Sarah decreed their banishment. At the age of 90, she became pregnant with Isaac, so called because she laughed at the news that she would be giving birth to a son (*Yitzhak*, i.e., Isaac, derives from the Hebrew root *tz-h-k*, "to laugh").

Rebekah, the daughter of Bethuel, son of Nahor, brother of Abraham, was the wife of Isaac, son of Abraham, and the second of the four Matriarchs. About 20 years after her wedding, she gave birth to twins, Esau and Jacob. She favored Jacob over Esau, and

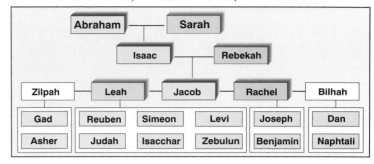

cunningly misled Isaac so he would bless Jacob with the blessing of the first-born, instead of his elder son, Esau.

Leah, the daughter of Laban, son of Bethuel, brother of Rebekah, was the third of the four Matriarchs. Jacob first married Leah instead of her sister Rachel, through her father's trickery. She bore Jacob six sons (Reuben, Simeon, Levi, Judah, Issachar, and Zebulun) and one daughter (Dinah). She gave to Jacob her handmaid Zilpah, who in turn bore Jacob two sons (Gad and Asher).

Rachel, the daughter of Laban, son of Bethuel, brother of Rebekah, was the last of the four Matriarchs and the beloved wife of Jacob. She was the mother of Joseph and Benjamin. She gave to Jacob her handmaid Bilhah, who bore Jacob two more sons (Dan and Naphtali). She died while giving birth to Benjamin and was buried in the way to Ephrath ("Rachel's Tomb").

The Exodus from Egypt and the Entry into Canaan
(Beginning of the 13th century — mid-13th century)

The route taken by the Israelites after their Exodus from Egypt, under the leadership of Moses, until their entry into the land of Canaan is not altogether clear, because most of the places and way stations described in the Bible have not been identified with certainty.

Migdol and Baal-zaphon, mentioned at the start of their journey, are known from Egyptian sources as fortresses at the northeastern edge of the Nile Delta. Because the Israelites did not choose the Way of the Sea (also called for a time the Way of the Philistines), along which Egyptian fortresses and way stations were scattered, they probably detoured this route from the south, in the area of the Red Sea, which they crossed on dry ground.

In the third month of the Exodus from Egypt there occurred the "revelation at Mount Sinai," in which the Law was given to the people of Israel through Moses.

In the wilderness of Sinai, the Israelites built a tabernacle (in Hebrew, *mishkan*)—the Tent of the Meeting, also known as the Tent of the Congregation—in which was placed the Ark of the Covenant, containing the stone tablets of the Law that were given to Moses during the Revelation on Mount Sinai. The portable tabernacle served as the focal center for God's work during the years of wandering in the wilderness and in the period of settlement in Canaan, until the building of Solomon's Temple in Jerusalem, to which the Ark of the Covenant and the rest of the Sanctuary's utensils were transferred.

The locations of the numerous way stations, through which the Israelites passed in their wanderings in the Sinai wilderness, are based on conjecture only. Only Kadesh-barnea has been identified with certainty—an oasis rich in springs, on the border of the Sinai and the land of Canaan. Kadesh-barnea was the focus of the

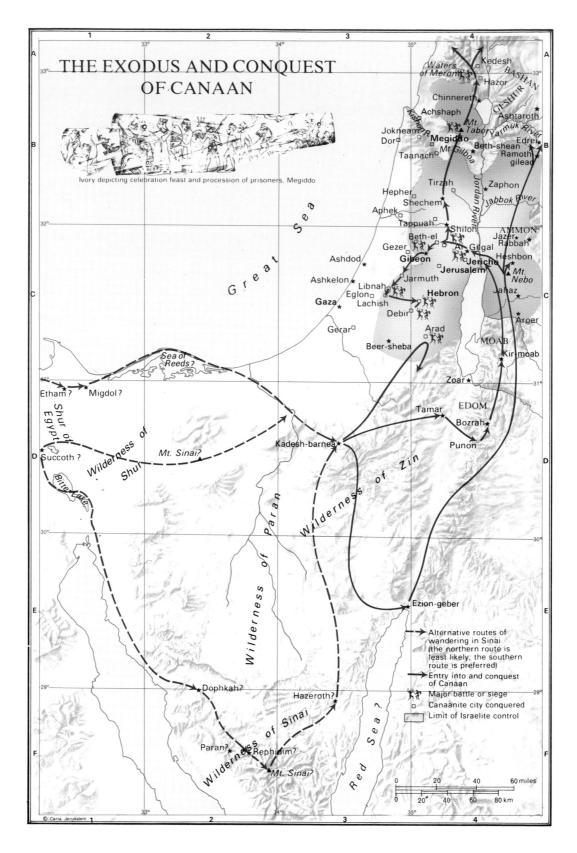

THE EXODUS AND CONQUEST
OF CANAAN

Ivory depicting celebration feast and procession of prisoners, Megiddo

→ Alternative routes of
wandering in Sinai
(the northern route is
least likely; the southern
route is preferred)

→ Entry into and conquest
of Canaan

⚔ Major battle or siege

□ Canaanite city conquered

▨ Limit of Israelite control

© Carta, Jerusalem

Israelites in their wanderings. From here the spies set out to scout the land of Canaan, and here the tribes organized their penetration into the land. The story of the spies is mainly linked to Hebron and its environs, but their final objective was actually Lebo-hamath, at the northern edge of Canaan.

The first attempt to invade the land of Canaan, which was made south of the Negeb and the Judean hills, failed as a result of strong resistance from the Negebites, the Canaanites and the Amalekites, headed by the king of Arad.

According to the Bible there were two routes by which the Israelites had penetrated the land of Canaan, both of which passed

through Transjordan. Settled in the southern sections of Transjordan were a number of nations close in origin to Israel—Edom, Moab, and Ammon—as well as the Amorite kingdom of Heshbon, which spread between Moab and Ammon. Sihon, the king of Heshbon, fought against the king of Moab and conquered the entire plain of Moab up to the river Arnon. Moses, wishing to take advantage of this situation, turned to the kings of Edom and Moab and requested permission for the Israelites to pass through their lands in order to reach the land of Sihon; but the kings of Edom and Moab refused, and Moses was forced to retreat as far south as Elath (Ezion-geber), bypassing Edom and Moab to the east, and

18

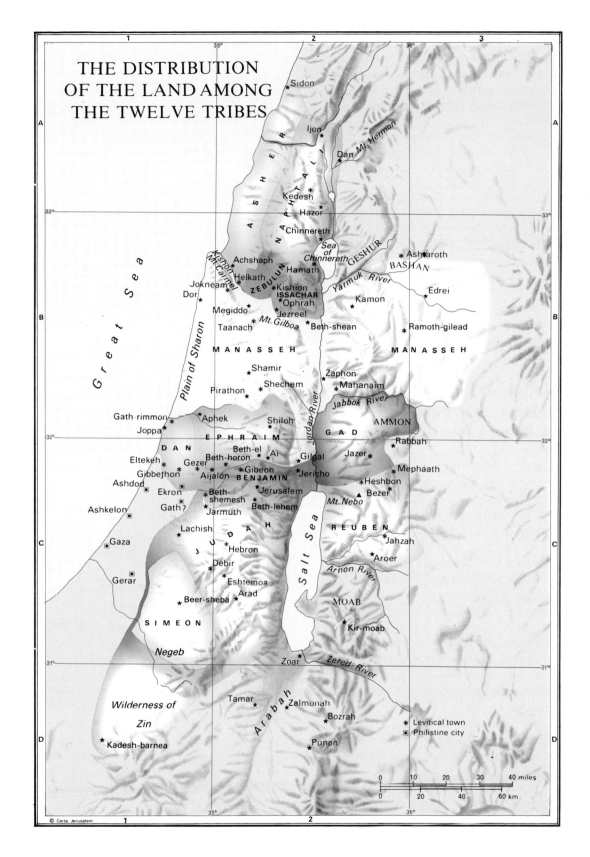

THE DISTRIBUTION
OF THE LAND AMONG
THE TWELVE TRIBES

*Sidon

Ijon

Dan Mt. Hermon

Kedesh

Hazor

Chinnereth

Sea
of
Chinnereth GESHUR *Ashtaroth

Achshaph Hamath BASHAN

Kishion Mt. Carmel ZEBULUN Helkath Edrei

Jokneam ISSACHAR Ophrah Kamon

Dor Megiddo Jezreel

Taanach Mt. Gilboa Beth-shean Ramoth-gilead

MANASSEH MANASSEH

Shamir Zaphon

Pirathon Shechem Mahanaim

Gath-rimmon Aphek Shiloh Jabbok River AMMON

Joppa EPHRAIM GAD

DAN Beth-el Ai Gilgal Jazer Rabbah

Eltekeh Beth-horon Gezer Jericho Mephaath

Gibbethon Aijalon Gibeon BENJAMIN Heshbon

Ashdod Ekron Beth- Jerusalem Bezer

Ashkelon Gath? shemesh Beth-lehem Mt. Nebo

Jarmuth REUBEN

Lachish JUDAH Salt Sea

Gaza Hebron Jahzah

Debir Aroer

Gerar Eshtemoa Arnon River

Beer-sheba Arad MOAB

SIMEON Kir-moab

Negeb

Zoar Zered River

Wilderness of
Zin Tamar Zalmonah

Bozrah *Levitical town

◻ Philistine city

Kadesh-barnea Punon

Arabah

0 10 20 30 40 miles

0 20 40 60 km

© Carta, Jerusalem

invade Sihon's kingdom from the wilderness of Kedemoth.

The other route, which is indicated from the list of wilderness stations, passes through the heart of Edom and Moab, reaching the plains of Moab, opposite Jericho.

The life and deeds of Moses end in the plains of Moab. The story dramatically recounts the elderly leader viewing from the top of Mount Nebo the land he so longed for and yet did not reach.

Moses was the son of Amram and Jochebed, of the tribe of Levi, and the leader of the Israelites in their Exodus from Egypt and in their wanderings in the wilderness. He received the Ten Commandments on Mount Sinai, also known as the Law of Moses. He is considered the progenitor of the Prophets. He is a central figure in the books of Exodus, Leviticus, Numbers, and Deuteronomy. According to the biblical narrative, he gained closer communion with God than any other man. He is also described as a military leader: he defeated Amalek, Sihon the Amorite, and Og, the king of Bashan, and endowed Israel with Transjordan. He himself was forbidden to enter the Promised Land, as punishment for disobeying God's command at Marah by smiting a rock to obtain water instead of speaking to it as he had been commanded. His burial place is unknown.

Aaron the High Priest was the son of Amram and Jochebed, of the tribe of Levi, the brother of Moses, his spokesman and right-hand aide in leading the Israelites through the wilderness. He succumbed to the demands of the multitude by making the golden calf. He was the first High Priest and progenitor of the priesthood. The priests, descended from Aaron the High Priest, are also known as "the sons of Aaron" or "the house of Aaron." He died on Mount Hor and, like Moses, was forbidden to enter the Promised Land because of disobeying God's command at Marah.

Joshua, the son of Nun, of the tribe of Ephraim, had served Moses since the time of his youth. He accompanied Moses on his ascent up to Mount Sinai. He led the warriors against Amalek and was one of the 12 spies sent by Moses to scout the land of Canaan. He became leader of the Israelites after Moses' death, during the period of conquest and settlement of the land, as related in the Book of Joshua. He conquered Jericho and Ai, and defeated the southern kings and the allied northern kings. After the conquest he divided the land of Israel among the tribes and turned Shiloh into a spiritual center. He was buried within his own allotment, at Timnath-serah.

The Conquest and Settlement

(Second half of the 13th century – 12th century)

The conquest of the land of Canaan is described in the books of Joshua and Judges. However, the versions are not always identical—the deeds of one tribe are occasionally ascribed to Israel as a whole, while the same acts attributed to Joshua are sometimes ascribed to one of the Judges as well. Events were given mostly partial, fragmentary descriptions or sometimes none at all. Moreover, the order of events remains somewhat obscure and, as a result, any descriptive survey is of necessity conjectural.

The conquest of the land of Canaan begins with the crossing of the river Jordan at Gilgal, but it should be noted that not all the tribes crossed the river. Some continued to move northward, in Transjordan, capturing the Amorite lands, where the tribes of Gad, Reuben, and the half-tribe of Manasseh remained and settled. Nevertheless, the main body of tribes did cross the Jordan westward and after capturing Jericho and Ai, they penetrated into the heart of the hill country.

The inhabitants of the land were Canaanite, mostly Semitic peoples, who are mentioned in the Bible in various connections: the Canaanites, the Hittites, the Hivites, the Perizzites, the Girgashites, the Amorites, and the Jebusites. They dwelled in independent city-states that sometimes banded together, primarily for the purpose of warring against a common enemy. In the beginning of the twelfth century, the land was invaded by a non-Semitic nation—the Philistines—who took control of the coastal area that was named after them, Philistia. Apparently, they were one of the Sea Peoples, a nation who had defeated the Hittite kingdom in the thirteenth and twelfth centuries; settled in Asia Minor, in the Aegean coastal area and in North Africa; and were almost destroyed by Rameses III, the king of Egypt, in 1170. The traces of their remains are scattered throughout the land of Israel.

The Bible describes the conquest of the land as a single campaign under the leadership of Joshua, son of Nun, a campaign that began with the capture of Jericho and that ended with the great battle against Jabin, the king of Hazor, by the Waters of Merom.

According to the Book of Joshua, the land of Canaan was conquered in stages. During the stage of penetration, Jericho and

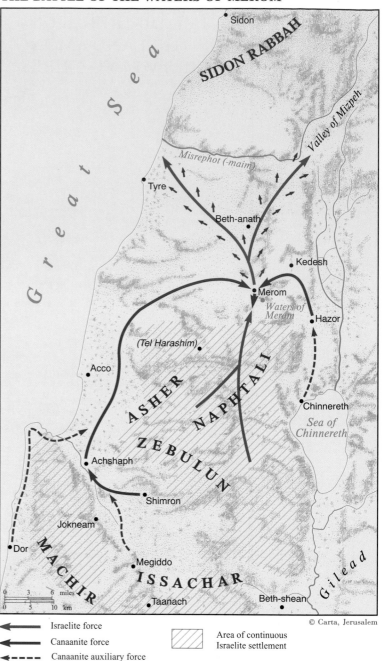

THE BATTLE OF THE WATERS OF MEROM

Israelite force
Canaanite force
Canaanite auxiliary force
Area of continuous Israelite settlement

© Carta, Jerusalem

Ai were captured, and a pact was made with the Gibeonites. The main event of the next stage was the battle of Gibeon. The Israelites rallied around Joshua to come to the aid of their allies, the Gibeonites, after the king of Jerusalem called up his allies to punish the Gibeonites for making a covenant with Israel. The Canaanite forces were routed, thereby creating conditions for the next stage—the rise of the southern tribes of Judah and Simeon. The tribes of Judah and Simeon probably came from the north, the Judahites settling in the Judean hills and the Simeonites, in the Shephelah (lowlands) and the Negeb. On the other hand, the Calebites and the Kenizzites, who were incorporated in the tribe of Judah, probably came from the south, capturing Hebron and Debir and settling in the area of Arad. The war of Deborah and the battle of the Waters of Merom—both aimed against the king of Hazor, Jabin—brought about the consolidation of the northern tribes.

In the twelfth century, at the end of the period of settlement of the tribes, the principal rival peoples in the land of Israel had become well established in their respective areas: the Canaanites in

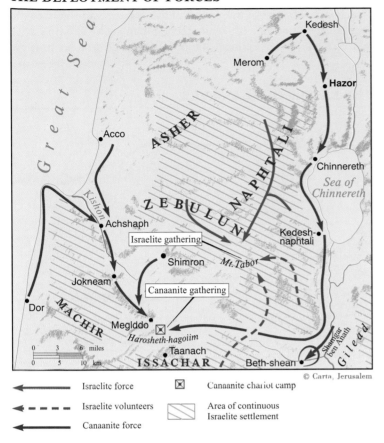

Israelite force — Canaanite chariot camp ⊠

Israelite volunteers - - - - — Area of continuous Israelite settlement

Canaanite force →

© Carta, Jerusalem

The Tribes of Israel

The twelve tribes of Israel, descendants of the sons of Jacob born to him by Leah and Rachel and Bilhah and Zilpah, are Reuben, Simeon, Levi, Judah, Issachar, Zebulun, Dan, Naphtali, Gad, Asher, Joseph, and Benjamin. The tribe of Joseph split into two tribes—Ephraim and Manasseh—resulting in the number of tribes actually reaching thirteen. Nevertheless, only twelve tribes were allotted territories in the land of Israel (the tribe of Levi, who earned its livelihood from donations and tithes received from the other tribes, did not receive a territory of its own and its cities were dispersed among the remaining tribal allotments).

The ties among the tribes after the period of settlement were rather weak, with their sole link found in the spiritual center they shared at Shiloh. Sometimes they did not join forces even when warring against a common enemy. Each tribe, or group of tribes, would for the most part fight separately. At times, they even fought among themselves, as, for example, in the days of Jephthah or following the incident of the "concubine in Gibeah" (Judg. 19–21). With the establishment of the monarchy, the differences among the tribes grew fainter, a process that was accelerated when the Assyrians exiled the ten northern tribes in the eighth century. The remaining remnants gathered in and around the area of Judah (the tribe of Simeon had already been incorporated in the tribe of Judah). Eventually, all the Israelites who did not assimilate into other nations were named "Jews." Only the tribe of Levi, because of its sacred status, kept its lineage.

The Period of the Judges
(12th – 11th centuries)

the northern valleys and plains, the Philistines on the southern coastal plain, and the tribes of Israel in the hill country and in Transjordan. The unconquered territories remained as foreign enclaves within the tribal allotments. The Book of Joshua calls the regions included within the borders of the Promised Land and not conquered during the period of settlement "the land that yet remains"—Philistia, in the south, and Phoenicia, Lebanon and the Lebanon valley, in the north.

The period of the Judges is the period between the death of Joshua and the establishment of the monarchy. The tribes of Israel continued to consolidate, each in their own territory, while the ties between them remained weak. The central sanctuary, which was located at Shiloh, within the tribal allotment of Ephraim, contained the Ark of the Covenant, the symbol of national unity, but its power as a unifying force was limited. The wars during this period were mainly ones against neighboring powers or incursors who

THE WAR OF EHUD

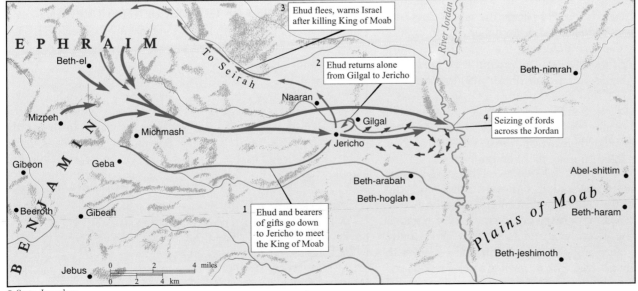

Israelite force →

Moabites - ◄ - ◄ -

© Carta, Jerusalem

THE WAR OF GIDEON

© Carta, Jerusalem

wanderings was the Ark returned to Kiriath-jearim, remaining there until King David brought it to Jerusalem.

A special chapter in the period of the Judges is the story of the three-year kingdom of Abimelech. Abimelech attempted to succeed his father, Gideon Jerubbaal, as ruler, and to turn his

THE BATTLE OF EBEN-EZER

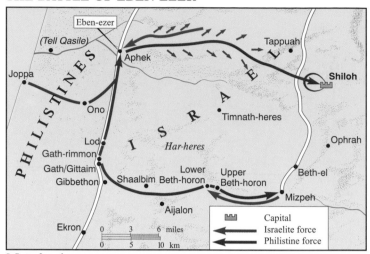

© Carta, Jerusalem

infiltrated the land to pillage and destroy. Under these conditions there developed a system of rule by local leaders who were called "Judges."

The judge was chieftain of a tribe, or of several neighboring tribes. Usually, he was called on to lead in an hour of great danger, and after he succeeded in overcoming the enemy and distancing the threat, he would be recognized as a leader even in times of peace, to "judge Israel." However, there were also judges who did not start out as war heroes. Recounted in the Book of Judges are Othniel, son of Kenaz; Ehud, son of Gera; Shamgar, son of Anath; Deborah the Prophetess; Gideon, son of Joash; Abimelech; Tola, son of Puah; Jair the Gileadite; Jephthah the Gileadite; Ibzan; Elon the Zebulunite; Abdon, son of Hillel; Samson; Eli the Priest; and Samuel the Prophet.

The "great" Judges, considered to be saviors, were Othniel, Ehud, Shamgar, Deborah the Prophetess, Gideon, Jephthah the Gileadite, Samson, and Samuel the Prophet. Othniel, Ehud, Gideon, and Jephthah fought mainly against the neighboring nations in Transjordan, who attempted to infiltrate Israel, and against desert marauders who would pillage the land's cities and produce. Othniel defeated the king of Aram-naharaim, an invader from Mesopotamia. Gideon defeated the Midianites. Ehud repelled the attempts of the Moabites to expand their borders at Israel's expense, and Jephthah repelled similar attempts made by the Ammonites.

The names of Shamgar, Samson and Samuel are associated with the wars against the Philistines, who dwelled along the southern coast of the land of Israel and who, because of their administrative and military superiority, attempted to subdue the tribes of Israel.

The most serious confrontation between Israel and the Philistines occurred in the mid-eleventh century, between Aphek and Eben-ezer, known as the "battle of Eben-ezer." The war ended with the defeat of the allied tribes of Israel. The Ark of the Covenant, which had been brought from Shiloh to the battlefield, fell into Philistine hands, and Shiloh itself was destroyed and ceased being a spiritual center. Only after some wonderful

leadership into a kingdom with the help of the Shechemites, who considered him one of their own because of his mother's lineage. However, the people of Shechem refused to accept his rule as king of Israel. Abimelech destroyed Shechem and died during the siege of Thebez.

The Book of Judges ends with the narrative of the "concubine in Gibeah." This is the story about the fraternal war between the tribe of Benjamin and the other Israelite tribes. The war was bloody and the tribe of Benjamin was almost completely annihilated. The tribe was returned to the fold and was restored only after a way had been found to provide wives for the remaining Benjaminites, who had fled to the wilderness "unto the rock Rimmon."

The last of the Judges was Samuel the Prophet, whose story is told in the biblical book named after him. He was also the only judge to be described as the leader of all Israel and symbolized the transition toward the establishment of the monarchy. He anointed King Saul, and afterward replaced him with King David.

THE WANDERINGS OF THE ARK OF THE COVENANT

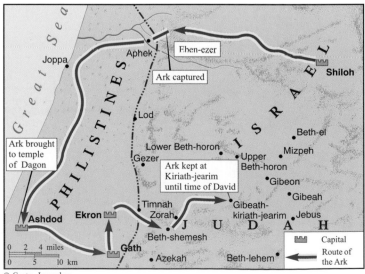

© Carta, Jerusalem

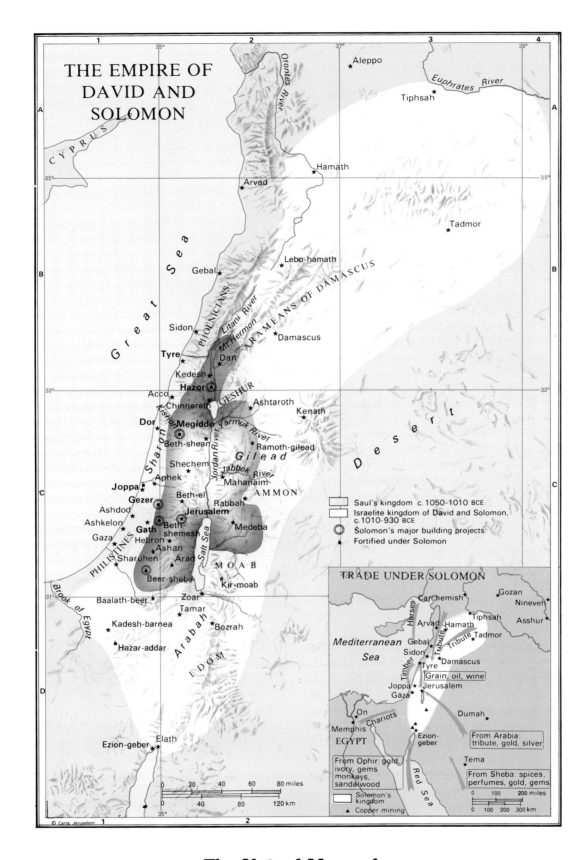

THE EMPIRE OF
DAVID AND
SOLOMON

Saul's kingdom c. 1050-1010 BCE
Israelite kingdom of David and Solomon, c.1010-930 BCE
Solomon's major building projects
Fortified under Solomon

TRADE UNDER SOLOMON

© Carta, Jerusalem

The United Monarchy

(End of 11th century – end of 10th century)

The United Monarchy is the term ascribed to the kingdom of Israel in the days of Kings Saul, David, and Solomon. Unlike the Judges before them and the kings of Judah and Israel after them, these three kings ruled over all the twelve tribes of Israel. The monarchy arose as a result of the people's demand to crown a king, apparently in order to cope with the Philistine threat. The United Monarchy lasted for about one hundred years and was divided after the death of Solomon.

Saul, the first king of Israel, was the son of Kish of the tribe of Benjamin. His reign is described in the Bible in three versions: in the beginning, he was secretly anointed king by Samuel the Prophet, then he was chosen (by the casting of lots) at Mizpeh to reign over the tribe of Benjamin, and, after the victory at Jabesh-gilead, he was coronated at Gilgal to rule over the whole of Israel. He reigned from approximately 1025 to 1006. Saul began with a war against the Philistines, driving them from the hill country and

THE KINGDOMS OF DAVID AND ESHBAAL

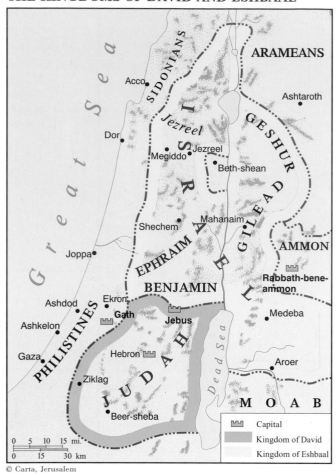

© Carta, Jerusalem

alliances at will. During his reign (1004–968), David completed Israel's war with the Philistines and defeated them, conquered Jerusalem from the Jebusites and made it the capital of Israel (1004), set up a monarchical regime and expanded its borders, organized the administration of the new state, and established a large, disciplined and well-equipped army. Apart from all this, he was also a spiritual man and a "sweet psalmist of Israel," as tradition has it. Apart from his lamentations about Saul and Jonathan and Abner, the son of Ner, tradition also accredits him as a psalmist. His image is inscribed in the people's consciousness as a symbol for a warrior who redeemed his people from the hands of their enemy, an admired king who established the Israelite monarchy, built Jerusalem, and brought security and glory to the nation.

Solomon succeeded his father David as king of Israel (968–928). The days of his reign and those of David are considered the Golden Age of the Israelite monarchy. He organized the kingdom and divided it into districts, built cities and fortresses, founded numerous enterprises and established commercial ties with states both near and far, and he built the Temple in Jerusalem. To finance all this, he imposed heavy taxes that caused increasing unrest among the people and brought about the division of the kingdom after his death. Tradition ascribes Solomon with the composition of the books of Proverbs, The Song of Songs, Ecclesiastes, and Psalm 72 in the Book of Psalms. His image, wealth and wisdom are praised in the Bible and in Jewish legend (and following that, also in Christian and in Muslim legend), and he was granted the epithet, "the wisest of all men."

continuing to fight them throughout his reign (until he was defeated at the battle of Gilboa). Saul also inflicted heavy defeats on the aggressive neighbors of Israel in the east (Ammon, Moab, Edom) and on Zobah in the north and Amalek in the south. Saul's victories lifted the people's spirit and laid the cornerstone for the mighty kingdom that was to follow.

Saul was the first to establish a regular Israelite army—3,000 soldiers in all—and to command them personally, or with the help of his son Jonathan. However, he was unable to consolidate all the tribes into a single nation. During the war with Amalek, a rift formed between Samuel and Saul, because Saul had spared King Amalek and not killed him as God commanded. Saul's situation became even more complicated in the war with David, as related in the Book of Samuel, in the beginning because of jealousy, and later because of a power struggle. Saul is described as a tragic figure given to volatile moods. When he was defeated at the battle with the Philistines on Mount Gilboa, he fell on his sword and died.

After Saul's death, the kingdom split in two for the first time: Abner, the son of Ner, proclaimed Eshbaal (Ish-bosheth), one of Saul's surviving sons, as king of Israel, at Mahanaim beyond the Jordan, while the elders of Judah proclaimed David as king, at Hebron. Eshbaal and David's kingdoms existed side by side for about two years (1006–1004), until David overpowered Eshbaal and combined the kingdoms of Israel and Judah into one.

David, the son of Jesse, is the founder of the Davidic dynasty— the House of David. He was already active in the days of Saul's kingdom. He fought Goliath, was appointed commander-in-chief by Saul, aroused Saul's wrath and jealousy, established for himself a private army of warriors, organized incursions, and broke off

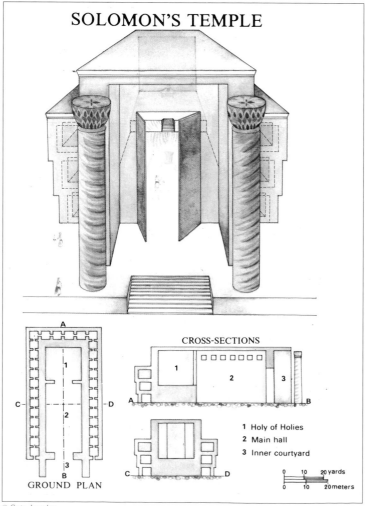

© Carta, Jerusalem

24

The Kingdom of Israel

The northern kingdom of Israel arose after the division of the United Monarchy of Israel. It embraced the tribal territories not included in the kingdom of Judah. It existed from 928 until the destruction of Samaria (in c. 722). During this period, it was ruled by kings of various dynasties. Jeroboam, the son of Nabat and founder of the kingdom, rebelled against King Solomon and, in the days of Solomon's son Rehoboam, was crowned at Shechem. He built royal sanctuaries at Beth-el, in the southern part of his kingdom, and at Dan in the north, in order to divert the ten tribes from their pilgrimage to the Temple in Jerusalem. There was constant friction between the kingdom of Israel and Aram in the north and with the kingdom of Judah in the south. Omri made Samaria his capital, made a covenant with Tyre, and introduced Baal worship to the land, which grew in the days of his son Ahab. The prophets (Elijah, Elisha, and Micaiah, the son of Imlah) zealously opposed Omri and Ahab. Together with Aram, Ahab succeeded in defeating the Assyrians in the battle of Qarqar (in 853) and his regnal years saw a period of prosperity. Jehu destroyed the House of Omri and cleansed the land of Baal worship. However, he lost the support of Tyre and was forced to pay a levy to Assyria in return for aid in his struggle with the Arameans. In the days of Jeroboam II, the kingdom of Israel enjoyed its second, and last, period of growth. Aram was repelled and the kingdom of Israel spread to the Bashan and the Golan and, in Aram, up to Lebo-hamath. The last kings of Israel were unable to halt the Assyrians' thrust toward Egypt. After two failed revolts, the kingdom of Israel was conquered by the Assyrians, who exiled some of the Israelites eastward, replacing them with inhabitants brought from other districts of the Assyrian kingdom (the Cuthites). The history of the kings of Israel is told mainly in the Book of Kings and in I Chronicles.

The Kings of Israel

928–907	Jeroboam (son of Nabat)
907–906	Nadab (son of Jeroboam)
906–883	Baasha
883–882	Elah (son of Baasha)
882	Zimri
882–871	Omri
871–851	Ahab (son of Omri)
851–850	Ahaziah (son of Ahab)
850–842	Jehoram/Joram (son of Ahab)
842–814	Jehu
814–800	Jehoahaz (son of Jehu)
800–785	Joash/Jehoash (son of Jehoahaz)
785–749	Jeroboam II (son of Jehoash)
749	Zechariah (son of Jeroboam)
748	Shallum
748–737	Menahem
737–735	Pekahiah (son of Menahem)
735–731	Pekah
731–722	Hoshea

The kings of Israel numbered 19—two from the house of Jeroboam, two from the house of Baasha, four from the house of Omri, five from the house of Jehu, two from the house of Menahem, and four individual kings.

Jeroboam, son of Nabat, was the first king of Israel (928–907) after the division of Solomon's kingdom. He served under Solomon and rebelled against him. When Solomon ordered him put to death, Jeroboam fled to Shishak, the king of Egypt. After Solomon's death, he was proclaimed king over the ten tribes, as prophesied by Ahijah the Shilonite. He made his capital at Shechem, then at Penuel beyond the Jordan, and finally at Tirzah. He reinstated cult worship of the two golden calves and established altars for them in Beth-el and Dan, after which pagan worship continued in the kingdom of Israel until its destruction. His kingdom suffered from incursions by the Egyptian king Shishak and from the hostile acts of Rehoboam and Abijah, the kings of Judah.

Nadab, son of Jeroboam, was king for two years (907–906). During the siege of the Philistine city of Gibbethon, Baasha, son of Ahijah, conspired against Nadab, had him put to death, and seized the throne.

Baasha, son of Ahijah, of the house of Issachar, was the third king of Israel (906–883). He rebelled against Nadab, the son of Jeroboam, destroyed his entire family, and seized the throne. Throughout his reign he battled against Asa, king of Judah, and for this purpose he allied himself with King Ben-hadad I of Aram-Damascus. However, Asa bribed Ben-hadad, who broke off his ties with Baasha.

Elah, son of Baasha, reigned for less than two years (883–882). He was killed by Zimri, one of his two commanders of the chariots, who tried to seize his throne after destroying the entire house of Baasha.

Zimri was the fifth sovereign of Israel (882). He was commander of half the chariots of Elah, and killed the king and his family in an attempt to gain the throne. When the army heard of Elah's murder, the soldiers proclaimed their general, Omri, king, who in turn marched his army against Zimri at Tirzah. The self-crowned Zimri retreated into the late king's palace, set it on fire, and perished in its ruins after only seven days of rule.

Omri was the sixth king of Israel (882–871) and founder of the Omri dynasty. He was an army general at the time of Elah's murder. After the murder, a revolt broke out over the rule between Omri, who was coronated by his army, and Tibni, the son of Ginath, whom "half the people" desired to raise to the throne. Omri prevailed and consolidated his rule. In the middle of his reign, he established Samaria, which was the capital of Israel until its fall. Omri made a covenant with Tyre and with the king of Judah, and in his time the kingdom of Israel stabilized and the political-military situation improved.

Ahab, son of Omri, the seventh king of Israel (871–851), continued the covenant with Tyre and married Jezebel, the daughter of Ethbaal, king of Tyre and the Sidonians. He made a covenant with Judah and married his daughter Athaliah to Jehoram, the son of Jehoshaphat king of Judah. He captured and returned to Israelite rule all the cities that had been taken by Aram. He headed the royal alliance against Shalmaneser III, king of Assyria, during the battle of Qarqar. Ahab fell in Ramoth-gilead, in the war with Aram. During Ahab's reign, Israel knew prosperity and growth, but the "incident of Naboth" and Ahab's benevolent attitude toward Baal worship raised the ire of the prophets, in particular, Elijah.

Ahaziah, son of Ahab and Jezebel, succeeded his father as king of Israel (851–850). The defeat of Israel by Aram, the attacks of King

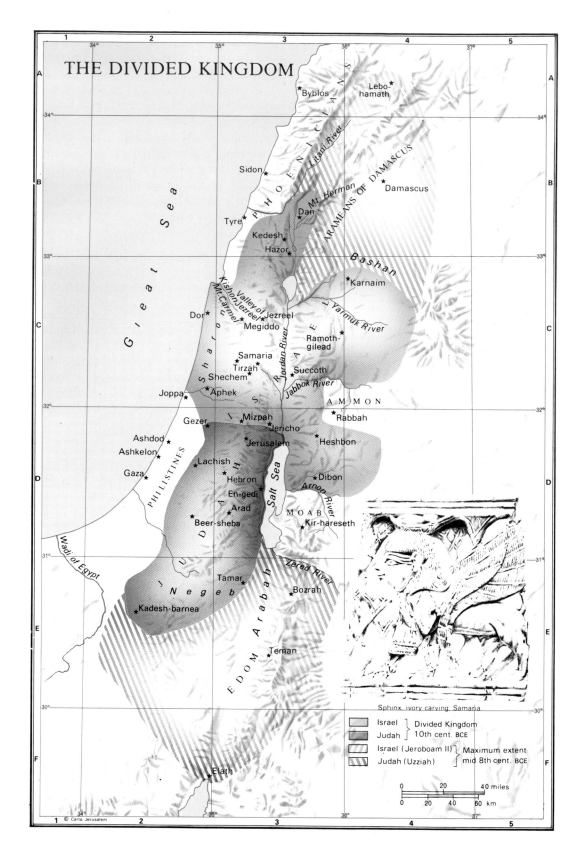

THE DIVIDED KINGDOM

Sphinx, ivory carving, Samaria

Israel	Divided Kingdom
Judah	10th cent. BCE
Israel (Jeroboam II)	Maximum extent
Judah (Uzziah)	mid 8th cent. BCE

0   20   40 miles
0   20   40   60 km

© Carta, Jerusalem

Mesha of Moab, and the weakening of the covenant made between Israel and Judah caused the weakened military and political situation in the kingdom of Israel during his reign. Baal worship continued to spread, apparently under the influence of his mother Jezebel. He was wounded in an accident and died of his injuries. Because he had no sons, his brother inherited the throne.

Jehoram/Joram, son of Ahab, ascended to the throne (850–842), succeeding his brother Ahaziah. With the help of Jehoshaphat, king of Judah, and the Edomite army, he defeated the invading army of Mesha, king of Moab. During his reign,

Hadad II, king of Aram, invaded Israel and besieged Samaria, but the Aramean army fled when the rumor spread that the Egyptian army was coming to the aid of Israel. Jehoram was wounded in the war with Hazael and returned to Israel to recuperate. Meanwhile, Jehu, his military minister, had been secretly anointed by command of the prophet Elisha. Jehu conspired against the king and had him killed.

Jehu, son of Jehoshaphat son of Nimshi, was founder of the Jehu dynasty and tenth king of Israel (842–814). He was a commander in King Jehoram's army, was anointed secretly by a disciple sent by the prophet Elisha, plotted against Jehoram, killing him and destroying the entire house of Ahab. He abolished Baal worship, but continued to practice the ritual of the golden calves, first instituted by Jeroboam, son of Nabat. He had the support of the army, the common people and the prophets, but was condemned by the prophet Hosea. He paid a levy to Shalmaneser III, king of Assyria, thereby avoiding a confrontation with King Hazael of Aram.

Jehoahaz was the son and successor of Jehu, and eleventh king of Israel (814–800). The period of his reign was a low point in Israel's history. Hazael, the king of Aram, invaded Israel and made Jehoahaz his subject and subject of his son Ben-hadad.

Joash/Jehoash, son of Jehoahaz, was the twelfth king of Israel (800–785). Taking advantage of the Assyrian king Adad-nirari's campaign against Aram, he attacked Aram and freed the kingdom of Israel from its yoke. He defeated Amaziah, king of Judah, in the battle between the army of Judah and the army of Israel, near Beth-shemesh, and took him prisoner. He invaded Jerusalem, looted the treasures of the king's palace and the Temple, razed sections of the city wall as a sign of surrender, and took away hostages.

Jeroboam (Jeroboam II), son of Jehoash, expanded and consolidated the kingdom of Israel as in the days of David and Solomon. His reign (785 749) was a period of prosperity and growth. In this respect he was counted among the great kings of Israel. Nevertheless, according to the Bible, he did evil in the eyes of God and the prophet Amos, who reproved him for the social woes and pagan worship that prospered under him, and predicted his doom. The prophets Hosea and Jonah also prophesied during his time.

Zechariah was the son of Jeroboam II. He reigned for about half a year (in 749), until he was murdered by Shallum, son of Jabesh. His murder marked the end of the Jehu dynasty.

Shallum, son of Jabesh, conspired against Zechariah, son of Jeroboam, king of Israel, killed him, and reigned for 30 days (in 748), until he was slain by Menahem, son of Gadi.

Menahem, son of Gadi, slew Shallum, son of Jabesh, and seized his throne (748–737). He paid a heavy tribute to Tiglath-pileser III, king of Assyria, and ruled for about ten years, until his death.

Pekahiah, son of Menahem, succeeded his father to the throne for two years (737–735), until he was murdered by his captain, Pekah, son of Remaliah, who seized the throne.

Pekah, son of Remaliah, was a captain of King Pekahiah of Israel. He conspired against his king, killed him, and seized the throne (735–731). He made a covenant with Rezin, king of Aram, against the kingdoms of Judah and Assyria. The armies of Israel and Aram invaded Judah and besieged Jerusalem. The situation changed with the appearance of Tiglath-pileser III in Galilee. He invaded the hills of Ephraim and posed a threat to Samaria. According to the Bible, Hoshea, son of Elah, conspired against Pekah, killed him, and seized the throne.

Hoshea, son of Elah, was the nineteenth and last king of Israel (731–722). He conspired against his king Pekah, son of Remaliah, killed him, and seized the throne. He paid a heavy tax to Tiglath-pileser III, king of Assyria, and during his reign, Assyria annexed most of the territory of the kingdom of Israel. For a time, Hoshea, apparently together with other allies, rebelled against Assyria, and discontinued the levy. Hoshea was arrested by Shalmaneser III, king of Assyria, Samaria was placed under siege and, after about three years, was captured. The conquest put an end to the kingdom of Israel.

The Kingdom of Judah

The southern kingdom of Judah arose after the division of the United Monarchy of Israel. It extended over the tribal allotments of Judah, Benjamin, and Simeon. The kingdom existed from 928 until the destruction of the First Temple (in 587). During this period, it was ruled by 20 kings, 19 of them from the House of David. The kingdom of Judah conducted continuous wars with the kingdom of Israel and sometimes even called for the help of foreign states. In general, it lost on the battlefield and, in the days of Amaziah, it even became a subject-nation of Israel. In the days of Jehoshaphat, Jehoram and Ahaziah, a covenant was made between the two brethren kingdoms. Judah reached the height of its greatness in the days of Uzziah, who built roads to the Mediterranean and the Red Sea, and fortified the land. In 722, Samaria fell to Assyria, marking the end of the kingdom of Israel. Judah too became a subject-nation of Assyria in the days of Ahaz, but rebelled against it in the days of Hezekiah. King Josiah, taking advantage of Assyria's decline in the days of Sennacherib, succeeded in expanding his kingdom northward and possibly even westward. During his rebellion Jerusalem was captured. Jehoiachin was exiled, and Zedekiah was crowned king. Zedekiah also rebelled and in suppressing the revolt, the Babylonians destroyed the First Temple and exiled thousands to Babylonia. The history of the kingdom of Judah is recounted in the Book of Kings and in II Chronicles.

The Kings of Judah

928–911	Rehoboam	758–742	Jotham
911–908	Abijah/Abijam	742–726	Ahaz
908–867	Asa	726–697	Hezekiah
867–851	Jehoshaphat	697–642	Manasseh
851 843	Jehoram/Joram	642–640	Amon
843–842	Ahaziah/Jehoahaz	640–609	Josiah
842–836	Athaliah	609–608	Jehoahaz
836–799	Joash/Jehoash	608–597	Jehoiakim/Eliakim
799–786	Amaziah	597	Jehoiachin
786–758	Uzziah	597–587	Zedekiah

There were 20 kings of Judah, all of whom belonged to a single dynasty—the House of David—with the exception of Athaliah, the daughter of Ahab, king of Israel, who married Jehoram, king of Judah, and seized the throne after the death of his son Ahaziah.

Rehoboam, the first king of Judah (928–911) after the division of Solomon's kingdom, was the son of Solomon and Naamah the Ammonitess. After Solomon's death, representatives of the tribes complained to Rehoboam about the burden of the heavy taxes they had to bear. His answer ("my father hath chastised you with whips, but I will chastise you with scorpions" [I Kg. 12:11]) raised the wrath of the people, and the kingdom split in two. Rehoboam built fortresses in the Shephelah (the lowlands) and around Jerusalem, and throughout his reign he was in battle with the king of Israel. Also during his reign, Shishak, king of Egypt, invaded Judah and plundered its cities.

Abijah/Abijam was the second king of Judah (911–908) and successor of his father Rehoboam. He battled against Jeroboam, son of Nabat, and captured several of his cities. According to the Book of Kings, he followed in his father's sinful ways; according to Chronicles, he endeavored to recover the kingdom of the Ten Tribes and to restore the centrality of the Temple in Jerusalem.

THE WARS OF AMAZIAH AND JOASH

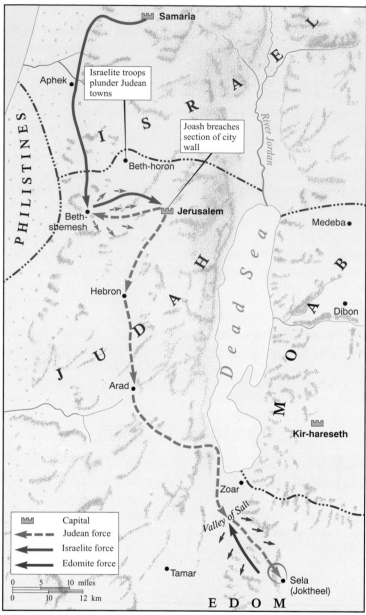

© Carta, Jerusalem

Asa succeeded his father Abijah and was the third king of Judah (908–867). Like his father, he also attempted to reunite Judah and Israel. He fought the house of Jeroboam and especially Baasha, but in the end he was defeated. He wished to cleanse the land of idol worship. He repelled the incursions of sheep and camel herdsmen, led by Zerah the Cushite, who were forced to retreat to the southern boundaries of Judah.

Jehoshaphat, son of Asa, was the fourth king of Judah (867–851). He fortified existing cities, established new ones, and strengthened his army. He imposed a levy on the Philistines, and defeated the Ammonite and Moabite armies. Toward the close of his reign, with the help of King Ahaziah of Israel, he built a navy designed to sail to Tarshish. His plan failed after the ships were wrecked at Ezion-geber.

Jehoram/Joram, the fifth king of Judah (851–843), was the eldest son of Jehoshaphat, his predecessor. He married Athaliah, daughter of Ahab, king of Israel, and Jezebel the Sidonian. Under her influence, he killed his six brothers and several of his ministers. The priestly city of Libnah rebelled against him, as did Edom. The prophet Elijah admonished him. The Philistines and Arabians

invaded Judah, plundered its property, and took Jehoram's wives and children hostage (only Ahaziah, the youngest son, was able to escape). He himself died of a serious illness, and was not buried in the Tombs of the Kings.

Ahaziah/Jehoahaz was the youngest son of Jehoram, king of Judah, and the only one to survive him. During his one-year reign (843–842), he followed the ways of his mother, Athaliah, in cult matters and reinforced the covenant with the house of Omri. He came to visit his uncle Jehoram, king of Israel, who had been wounded in war, and was killed in his flight from Jehu, who seized the rule in Israel.

Athaliah was the daughter of King Ahab of Israel and Jezebel the Sidonian. She married Jehoram, king of Judah, and persuaded him to kill his brothers and to go to war against Aram. After the death of her son Ahaziah, she killed all the possible inheritors to the throne and seized it herself (842–836). Jehosheba, Ahaziah's sister, succeeded in hiding her nephew Joash for six years, and in the seventh year, he was anointed king by the high priest Jehoiada. Athaliah was killed while trying to flee.

Joash/Jehoash, son of Ahaziah, was the eighth king of Judah (836–799). For six years he was concealed by his aunt Jehosheba, wife of the high priest Jehoiada, in order to save him from the hands of his grandmother, Athaliah, who had killed all his brothers and seized the throne. Joash was coronated by Jehoiada and the Davidic dynasty was renewed. In the days of Joash, the priestly status was reinforced, Jerusalem was cleansed of Baal worship, and the Temple was restored. Toward the close of his reign, he surrendered to Hazael, king of Aram, and was forced to send him the treasures from his palace and the Temple. He was murdered by conspirators from among his servants after the murder of Zechariah, the son of Jehoiada, who ordered the assassination.

Amaziah, son of Joash, was the ninth king of Judah (799–786). He punished the murderers of his father but did not harm their sons. He established an army for war with Edom and requested the participation of Israel's army, but abandoned that plan. After his victory over Edom, the strife between Judah and Israel grew. He declared war on Joash, king of Israel, was defeated and fell into captivity, and Jerusalem was captured and its treasures from the king's palace and the Temple were looted. During the last years of his reign, a breach apparently formed between him and the clan leaders, and Amaziah was murdered after his flight to Lachish.

Uzziah, son of Amaziah, was the tenth king of Judah (786–758). He was crowned king after his father's murder, and continued his policy of reinforcing Judah. He controlled several Philistine cities, fortified Jerusalem, built fortifications in Judah, and strengthened his army. Following his achievements, he wished to also assume the crown of the priesthood and, according to the narrative in Chronicles, he became afflicted with leprosy. Apparently, while still alive he placed his son Jotham in power, but it is not known precisely how many years before Uzziah's death this occurred. The prophets Isaiah, Amos and Hosea were active during his time.

Jotham succeeded his father Uzziah and was eleventh king of Judah (758–742). According to some calculations, he was regent also during the lifetime of his father, who was afflicted with leprosy, and perhaps did not rule independently. Jotham continued his father's policies: he fortified Jerusalem, established fortified cities and fortresses in Judah, apparently also ruled over Elath (Ezion-geber), subdued the Ammonites, and expanded the border of Judah eastward. At the close of his reign, Rezin, king of Aram, and Pekah, king of Israel, began to plot against Judah.

Ahaz was the son of Jotham and king of Judah (742–726). Part of his rule was as regent under his father and perhaps even his grandfather, Uzziah. He refused to join forces with Aram and Israel against Assyria. Aram and Israel attacked Judah and besieged Jerusalem. Against the advice of the prophet Isaiah, he turned to the Assyrian king Tiglath-pileser III for aid. He reinstated Aramean forms of cult worship in Jerusalem. At the time of his conflict with Aram and Israel, the Edomites and Philistines bit off chunks of territory from the kingdom of Judah, in the Negeb and in the western Judean hills.

Hezekiah was the son of Ahaz and king of Judah (726–697). He inherited a kingdom that was subject to Assyria. Under the guidance of the prophet Isaiah, he purified the Temple and abolished pagan worship. With the help of his allies, he rebelled against Assyria. Sennacherib, king of Assyria, defeated the allied armies, and Hezekiah surrendered and paid a heavy penalty. After Senna-cherib left, Hezekiah rebelled again. The Assyrian army besieged Jerusalem but left because of a plague. Against the advice of Isaiah, Hezekiah made a covenant with Merodach-baladan, king of Babylon and Sennacherib's enemy.

Manasseh was the son of Hezekiah and Hephzi-bah, and king of Judah (697–642). He was coronated at the age of 12 and reigned for 55 years—more than any other king of Judah. He built altars for Baal and Astarte and passed his son through fire, for Molech. The books of Kings and Jeremiah recount only his abominations. The Book of Chronicles relates how he was taken captive by an Assyrian king, prayed to God and repented for his sins, returned to his kingdom and remedied all.

Amon was the son of Manasseh and king of Judah. He followed in the ways of his father and, according to the narrative in Chronicles, was worse than Ahaz and Manasseh. He ruled for two years (642–640) and was murdered in a conspiracy by his courtiers. The people avenged him by putting all the conspirators to death, and secured the succession to his youngest son, Josiah.

Josiah was the son of Amon and king of Judah. He was coronated at the age of eight, and his regnal years (640–609) are considered the last Golden Age in the history of Judah. In his days the book of the Law of the Lord (i.e., Deuteronomy), which was stored deep inside the Temple, was found, he destroyed the pagan altars, reinstated the Divine service, made Jerusalem the single religious center, and led a religious revival movement. The decline of Assyria paved open the way for national independence, too, and Josiah was the only king of Judah who set out against Egypt. He was wounded and died while attempting to block the path of the army of Pharaoh Necho, king of Egypt, who attacked Assyria.

Jehoahaz was the son of Josiah and king of Judah. He reigned for only three months (in 609–608). Pharaoh Necho took him prisoner and brought him to Egypt, where he died.

Jehoiakim/Eliakim was the son of Josiah and king of Judah (608–597). He was coronated by Pharaoh Necho after the latter deposed his brother, Jehoahaz. He was a tyrant and wicked man who oppressed his people and persecuted Jeremiah and anyone else who predicted for him hard and difficult times. At the start of his reign, Judah was a subject-nation of Egypt, and after the battle of Carchemish, it became subject to Babylon. Jehoiakim rebelled against the Babylonian king Nebuchadnezzar. In the end, Nebuchadnezzar ascended upon Jerusalem, forcing its surrender. According to the Book of Chronicles, Jehoiakim was bound in fetters and carried off to Babylon.

THE CONQUESTS OF JOASH AND JEROBOAM II

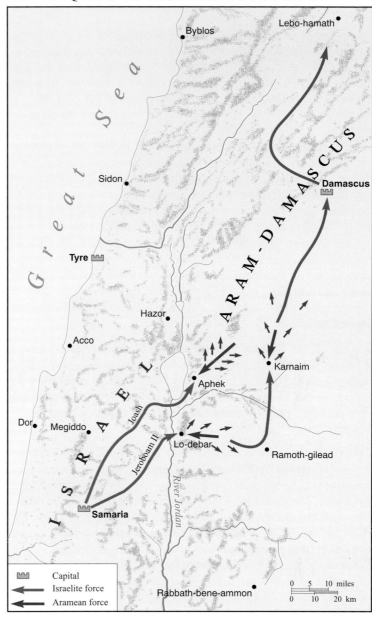

© Carta. Jerusalem

Jehoiachin, successor of his father Jehoiakim and king of Judah, rose to the throne during the rebellion against Babylon. He reigned for three months (in 597), until Nebuchadnezzar exiled him to Babylon along with his mother, members of his family, his ministers, and ten thousand soldiers. His life was spared and he remained in Nebuchadnezzar's court prison, until he was released in the days of Evil-Merodach, the Babylonian king's successor. From among his descendants arose the leaders during the Babylonian exile and the Return to Zion.

Zedekiah was the third son of Josiah and Hamutal, and the last king of Judah (597–587). He was coronated in the days of Nebuchadnezzar, who, on the same occasion, changed his name from Mattaniah to Zedekiah. Zedekiah was persuaded to rebel against Babylon, despite the warnings of the prophet Jeremiah. Nebuchadnezzar's army invaded Judah, besieged Jerusalem, and breached its walls. Zedekiah escaped but he was caught by the Chaldeans. His sons were slaughtered before his eyes, his own eyes were then blinded, and he was bound in fetters and brought to Babylon, where he died.

The Prophets

The prophet of the Bible was an emissary of God and the intermediary between the Divine Will and individuals, people, or the Gentile nations. His mission was forced upon him: he was chosen to be a prophet, sometimes against his will. In some instances in the Bible, the prophet is called either "a seer," "a visionary" or a "man of God," all of which are identical in meaning.

The sages listed 48 prophets and seven prophetesses, beginning with the patriarchs Abraham, Isaac and Jacob, and ending with Malachi, in the days of the Return to Zion. However, only the prophecies relevant to future generations are included in the Bible. The sages also counted seven prophets who prophesied to the Gentile nations, among them Balaam and Job.

The division between the Former Prophets and the Latter Prophets is designated by the order of their appearance in the Bible. Based on their character, status and deeds, the prophets can be divided into three categories, a division that also fits the periods of their activity: the "leader" prophets, the court prophets, and the classical prophets.

The first of the **"leader" prophets** was Moses. Miriam, the sister of Moses, was called a prophetess. Among the Judges were a few prophet-soothsayers, but only Deborah was called a prophetess. In the period of the Judges there were bands of prophets, but these were probably groups formed for their own purposes. Samuel was the last "leader" prophet.

Court prophets were active in the days of David and Solomon and in the days of the Divided Monarchy of Judah and Israel. Gad and Nathan were court prophets in the days of David and Solomon. The "man of God" Shemaiah and the "seer" Iddo recorded the chronicles of Rehoboam and Abijah. Ahijah the Shilonite, Jehu, son of Hanani, and Micaiah, son of Imlai, opposed the deeds of their kings and prophesied their doom. Elijah and Elisha were prophets who were forceful and decisive in their opinions and deeds, and they interfered in political, social and religious matters. The advice of Huldah the Prophetess was required by Josiah, king of Judah.

Classical prophets are the literary prophets: each one is associated with a book counted with the books of the Bible. Three of these are books of the Major Prophets (Isaiah, Jeremiah, and Ezekiel) and twelve are books of the Minor Prophets. The classical prophets are distinguished also for their religious fervor, their moral and social views, their historical outlook, and their power of rhetoric. They were not in need of fortune-telling or miraculous deeds, which were a separate part of the work of the Former Prophets.

Below are short biographies of the court prophets (the classical prophets are mentioned above in connection with the books named after them; see above, "The Books of the Bible").

Gad was a court prophet in the days of David. He joined David's regiment before David was king. David turned to him for God's advice. On the prophet's advice, David built an altar for God on the threshing floor of Araunah.

Nathan was a court prophet in the days of David and Solomon. He promised the House of David an eternal monarchy. He notified David about the postponement of building the Temple until the days of Solomon. He reproved David for the act of Bathsheba and Uriah (the parable of "the poor man's lamb"; II Sam. 12:1–4).

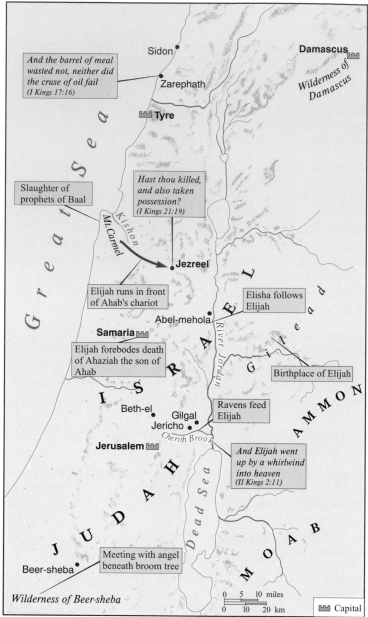

THE WANDERINGS OF ELIJAH

And the barrel of meal wasted not, neither did the cruse of oil fail (I Kings 17:16)

Slaughter of prophets of Baal

Hast thou killed, and also taken possession? (I Kings 21:19)

Elijah runs in front of Ahab's chariot

Elisha follows Elijah

Elijah forebodes death of Ahaziah the son of Ahab

Birthplace of Elijah

Ravens feed Elijah

And Elijah went up by a whirlwind into heaven (II Kings 2:11)

Meeting with angel beneath broom tree

Wilderness of Beer-sheba

0   5   10 miles
0   10   20 km

Capital

Sidon · Damascus · Zarephath · Tyre · Great Sea · Wilderness of Damascus · Mt. Carmel · Kishon · Jezreel · Abel-mehola · Samaria · River Jordan · Gilead · ISRAEL · AMMON · Beth-el · Gilgal · Jericho · Cherith Brook · Jerusalem · JUDAH · Dead Sea · MOAB · Beer-sheba

© Carta, Jerusalem

Ahijah the Shilonite was a prophet in the days of Solomon and Jeroboam. He was among the prophets who opposed Solomon because of the burden his heavy taxes imposed and because of the pagan cults he allowed to exist. He prophesied Jeroboam's reign over Israel, and realized his prophecy in a symbolic manner (he had rent Jeroboam's garment into 12 strips, gave ten to Jeroboam and left one for the House of David).

Shemaiah was "a man of God" in the days of Rehoboam, king of Judah. He passed on God's word of warning to the king not to go to war with Jeroboam, son of Nabat. He and the "seer" Iddo recorded the chronicles of Rehoboam and his wars.

Iddo was a "seer" in the days of Rehoboam and Abijah, kings of Judah. He recorded the chronicles of Rehoboam (with Shemaiah) and those of Abijah.

Jehu, son of Hanani, was a prophet in the days of Baasha, king of Israel, and Jehoshaphat, king of Judah. He reproved Baasha for his evil deeds and prophesied his doom.

Elijah the Prophet (also called "the Tishbite" and "the Gileadite") was a popular and powerful prophet, who lived in

THE ACTIVITIES OF ELISHA

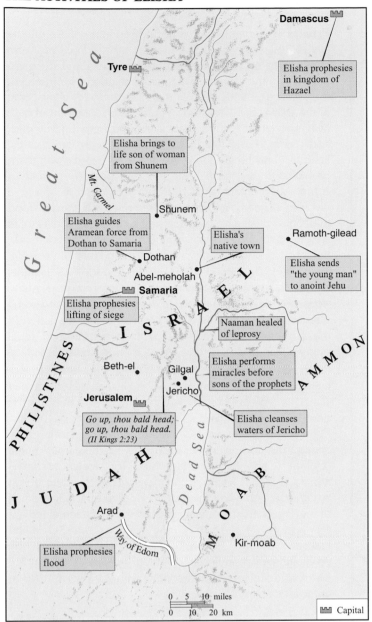

Damascus

Elisha prophesies in kingdom of Hazael

Tyre

Great Sea

Mt. Carmel

Elisha brings to life son of woman from Shunem

Shunem

Elisha guides Aramean force from Dothan to Samaria

Elisha's native town

Ramoth-gilead

Dothan

Elisha sends "the young man" to anoint Jehu

Abel-meholah

Samaria

Elisha prophesies lifting of siege

I S R A E L

Naaman healed of leprosy

Beth-el

Gilgal

Elisha performs miracles before sons of the prophets

AMMON

Jericho

Jerusalem

Go up, thou bald head; go up, thou bald head. (II Kings 2:23)

Elisha cleanses waters of Jericho

J U D A H

Dead Sea

M O A B

Arad

Way of Edom

Kir-moab

Elisha prophesies flood

PHILISTINES

```
0    5   10 miles
0   10   20 km
```

🏰 Capital

© Carta, Jerusalem

Elisha, son of Shaphat, was a prophet in the kingdom of Israel in the days of Kings Jehoram, Jehu, Jehoahaz, and Joash. Elijah cast his mantle on Elisha, thus anointing him prophet. He was active in political life, forceful in his opinions, and brave in his acts. He prophesied to the Israelite monarchy, on his command Jehu was anointed, he led the soldiers of Aram from Dothan to Samaria, and prophesied the lifting of the siege of Samaria. Many stories and miraculous deeds are associated with him: the story of the 42 children who were preyed upon by two bears ("Go up, thou bald head; go up, thou bald head"), the resurrection of the son of a

THE CITIES OF THE PROPHETS

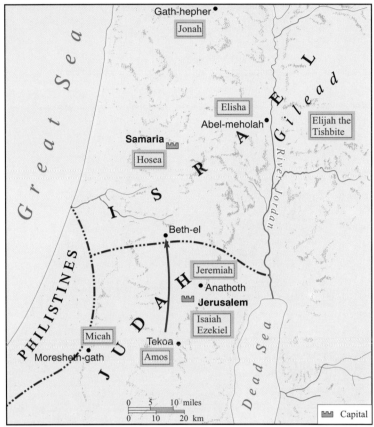

Gath-hepher

Jonah

Great Sea

Elisha

Abel-meholah

Elijah the Tishbite

Samaria

Hosea

I S R A E L

Gilead

River Jordan

PHILISTINES

Beth-el

Jeremiah

Anathoth

Jerusalem

Micah

Moresheth-gath

Tekoa

Amos

Isaiah Ezekiel

J U D A H

Dead Sea

```
0    5   10 miles
0   10   20 km
```

🏰 Capital

© Carta, Jerusalem

---

the kingdom of Israel and was active in the days of Kings Ahab and Ahaziah. He was a zealot for the belief in one God and fought vigorously against Baal worship. He was pursued in the days of the monarchy and often sought refuge in hiding places, but he would return in times of need. He argued with the prophets of Baal and had them slaughtered. He performed miracles and experienced miracles himself: the ravens fed him, he resurrected a dead boy, stopped the rain, and went up by a whirlwind into heaven. He consecrated Elisha as his disciple and, upon his instructions, Hazael was proclaimed king over Aram and Jehu, king over Israel. Already in the days of Malachi, the belief spread that Elijah would return before the Day of Judgment. Many legends are woven around him, among them the legend that he would herald the coming of the Messiah. During the seder on Passover eve, it is customary to place a cup of wine in his honor ("Elijah's cup").

Micaiah, son of Imlah, was a prophet in the days of Ahab, king of Israel, and Jehoshaphat, king of Judah. Ahab despised him because he always prophesied his doom. After one of his harsh prophecies, Zedekiah, son of Chenaanah and one of the false prophets under Ahab, rose and struck his face, and sent him to prison.

Shunammite woman, the cure of Naaman from leprosy, purifying the waters of Jericho, and more.

Huldah was a prophetess in the days of Josiah, king of Judah. Hilkiah, Ahikam, and Abdon turned to her upon the king's request to demand God's word, and upon her advice, the king acted.

The Latter Prophets by their periods: Amos and Hosea prophesied during the Israelite monarchy, in the eighth century, before its destruction. Isaiah, Joel, Micah, Nahum, Habakkuk, Zephaniah, and Jeremiah prophesied during the Judahite monarchy. Obadiah prophesied after the destruction, Ezekiel prophesied during the exile of Judah, and Haggai, Zechariah, and Malachi prophesied after the Return to Zion.

False prophets arose in Israel alongside the prophets of God. They misled the people for the sake of monetary gain, and were among those who preached Baal and Astarte worship. Jezebel of Tyre had installed the prophets of Baal and of Astarte. In the Book of Nehemiah, a false prophetess is also mentioned—Noadiah of Sanballat's community—who incited against Nehemiah.

THE LEVITICAL CITIES

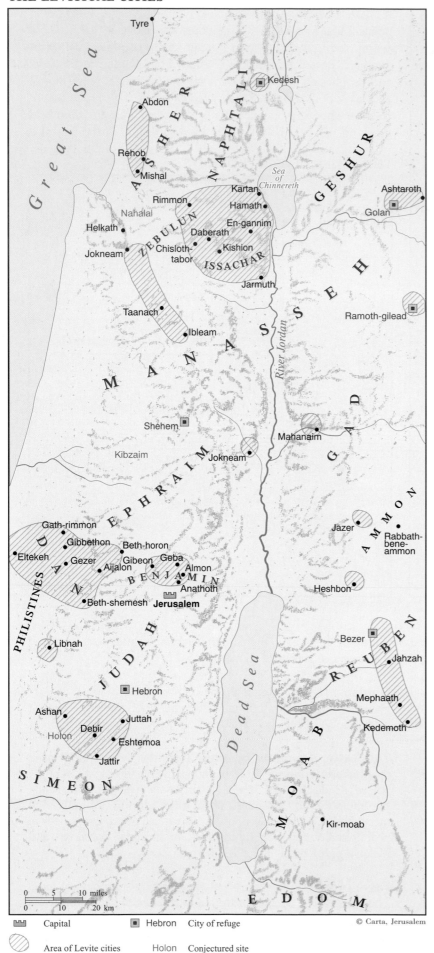

Capital   ■ Hebron   City of refuge

Area of Levite cities   Holon   Conjectured site

© Carta, Jerusalem

The Priests, Levites, and Israel

Priests (*kohanim*) were male descendants of Aaron the High Priest, brother of Moses, of the tribe of Levi, and were consecrated to serve in the priesthood of the Tabernacle and later in the Temple. Their tasks included the offering of the sacrifices, the burning of the incense, and the arranging of the shewbread. They did not receive an allotment of their own since they earned their livelihood from priestly gifts, such as parts of sacrifices, firstborn flocks and cattle, firstfruits, and tithes. Their status also imposed upon them prohibitions and restrictions, such as being forbidden to come into contact with a dead person or to marry a divorced woman. At the head of the priestly hierarchy stood the High Priest, whose special duties included the Temple service on the Day of Atonement (Yom Kippur). Essentially, the priest's duties were confined to matters of worship. However, in the period of the Judges and the First Temple, he was assigned additional responsibilities: he conveyed the word of God to the nation; he was approached regarding queries to God; he was a teacher instructing the nation in the Torah; he rendered judgment on questions of ritual purity and impurity; and he served as judge in legal matters.

(In the days of the Second Temple, the High Priests became political leaders but, as a consequence, lost their status as interpretors of Jewish law, as teachers of the people, and as spiritual guides. Today, only a few distinguishing signs of the *kohanim* remain: guarding their lineage, as, for example, expressed in the family name [Cohen, Cahane, Katz (acronym for *kohen tzedek—righteous priest*), etc.]; reciting the priestly blessing in the synagogue; and being the first to be called up to the reading of the Torah. Of the priestly gifts, all that have remained are the custom of redeeming the firstborn male child [in Hebrew, *pidyon ha-ben*] and, in holy matters, the prohibition of marrying a divorced woman. *Kohanim* are also forbidden to come in contact with the deceased or to enter a cemetery.)

Levites are members of the Levite tribe not included in the order of priests. Like the priests, they were chosen by Moses to serve in the Tabernacle as a reward for their loyalty to him regarding the golden calf. During the wanderings in the wilderness, they were charged with carrying the Tabernacle and its holy vessels, and helping the priests. During the period of settlement in Canaan, the Levites did not receive territories of their own but were allotted 48 cities, and subsisted from the tithes they received from the people. When the First Temple was built and the wanderings of the Tabernacle ceased, the Levites were divided into 24 watches that they served in the Temple, coinciding with the 24 watches of the priests. Among the Levites were appointed judges, officials, public teachers of the Torah, and scribes.

(In the Second Temple period, their duties in the Temple [and later in the synagogue] were confined to those of singers, musicians, gatekeepers, and public servants. The Levites were ranked second to the priests in the social hierarchy, and above the rank of Israel. Some of them have also kept their lineage through their family names—Levi, Halevi, Levine, Leviteh, etc.)

Israel refers to a Jew who is neither a priest nor a Levite.

THE CLOSING YEARS OF THE KINGDOM OF JUDAH

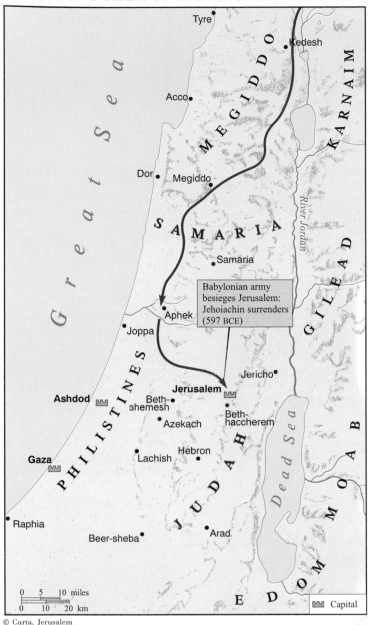

Babylonian army besieges Jerusalem: Jehoiachin surrenders (597 BCE)

© Carta, Jerusalem

The Destruction and Exile

Exile refers to the banishment of the people of Israel from their land and their resettlement in foreign lands. In the "reproof section" of the Bible (Lev. 26; Deut. 28–30), exile is mentioned as the gravest of all punishments the people of Israel could expect if they did not observe God's commandments. However, the exiles are promised to return to their land if they repent for their evil ways.

It is customary to list a number of exiles in the history of Israel. **Egyptian exile**, when all the Jewish people dwelled among a foreign nation in enslavement. **Assyrian exile:** the exile of the northern tribes of Israel and those living in the cities along the Jordan by King Tiglath-pileser of Assyria in 733. After some 12 years, King Sargon of Assyria captured Samaria and exiled the rest of the tribes (only the kingdom of Judah remained). **Babylonian exile:** in 597, Nebuchadnezzar, king of Babylon, exiled King Jehoiachin and all his ministers and soldiers from Jerusalem, and coronated his uncle Zedekiah instead. Zedekiah also rebelled against Babylon, and Nebuchadnezzar returned and ascended upon Jerusalem. In c. 587, the city was destroyed, the Temple was burned, and many more Judahites were exiled to Babylon.

(The term "exile" is also used for the "exiles" of Zion after the destruction of the Second Temple. For example, the Edomite exile is the name for the enslavement of Israel by the Romans; the Ishmaelite exile—name for the exiles of Israel in the Islamic countries; the Spanish exile—expulsion of the Jews from Spain and Portugal at the end of the fifteenth century CE; and, in general, the dispersion of the majority of the Jewish people in the Diaspora, outside Israel.)

The Return to Zion

The Return to Zion refers to the return of some of the Babylonian exiles to the land of Israel following the decree of Cyrus in 538. The returnees left in summer and before the Hebrew month of Tishri, they established the altar and instituted the sacrificial service. In the second year in the Hebrew month of Iyyar, the construction of the Temple began. The first group of returnees arrived under the leadership of Zerubbabel and numbered 42,360 people. The list of returnees included descendants of the families who had been exiled to Babylon. Close to the mid-fifth century, with the

THE EXILE FROM JUDAH

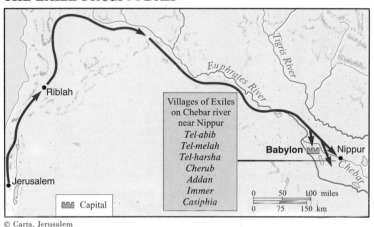

Villages of Exiles on Chebar river near Nippur

Tel-abib
Tel-melah
Tel-harsha
Cherub
Addan
Immer
Casiphia

© Carta, Jerusalem

THE FINAL COMPAIGN OF NEBUCHADNEZZAR AGAINST JUDAH

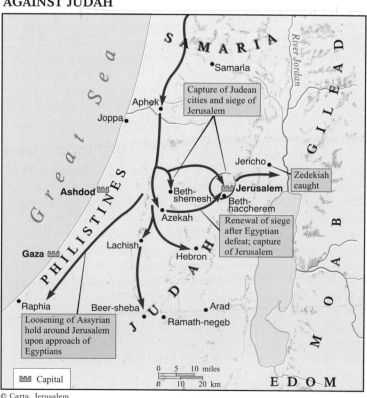

Capture of Judean cities and siege of Jerusalem

Zedekiah caught

Renewal of siege after Egyptian defeat; capture of Jerusalem

Loosening of Assyrian hold around Jerusalem upon approach of Egyptians

© Carta, Jerusalem

Map labels: Great Sea, Shechem, Aphek, Joppa, SAMARIA, Plain of Ono, Ono, Neballat, Lod, Hadid, Hazor, River Jordan, Gedor, Beth-el, Ayyah, Mizpeh, Michmash, Ramah, Geba, Gezer, Chephirah, Gibeon, Azmaveth, Jericho, Tyrus, Kiriath-jearim, Nob, Anathoth, Beeroth, YEHUD, Ananiah, Zorah, Jerusalem, Zanoah, Beth-haccherem, Ashdod, ASHDOD, Beth-lehem, Netophah, Ashkelon, Azekah, Adullam, Tekoa, Keilah, Beth-zur, Mareshah, Dead Sea, MOAB, Lachish, Hebron, AMMON, Gaza, Besor Brook, IDUMEA, En-gedi, Ziklag, Beth-pelet, Jeshua, Arad, Beer-sheba, Moladah

0 2 4 miles
0 5 10 km

© Carta, Jerusalem

Legend:
Capital
Gedor District capital

second return, under Ezra, about 5,000 people arrived. Altogether, about half of Babylonian Jewry had returned.

The building of the Temple began in 520 and was completed in 515. The costs of the sacrifices were borne by the authorities. The hardships of absorbing such a large migration and the sparse number of residents in the land strengthened the rule of the upper classes and increased the social tension. The shortage of women among the returnees (the first return included 30,000 men and only 12,000 women and children) resulted in many mixed marriages. The prophet Malachi complained of this phenomenon, and the Book of Ezra reveals that this custom even extended to priestly circles. Close to the return of Ezra, Nehemiah (who some predate to Ezra) arrived to build the walls of Jerusalem. He, like Ezra, was alert to social and religious reforms.

The returnees at first settled in the vicinity of Jerusalem, in an area whose size was only a fifth of the former kingdom of Judah. They found here a sparse Jewish community. It was these returnees who determined the character of Jewish settlement in the land, according to the modes of life they had adopted for themselves in Babylon. The national framework uniting the nation into a single unit had somewhat the character of a religious community, especially in its segregation. Aramaic was the official language of the Persian kingdom, and it was the language to which the returnees from Babylon were accustomed. In the same period, the Aramaic script was apparently adapted to the Hebrew one and gradually replaced the ancient Hebrew script, although the latter was not discarded completely. Similarly, this also occurred in the realm of the spoken word and ever since, Aramaic and Hebrew have been used side by side.

34

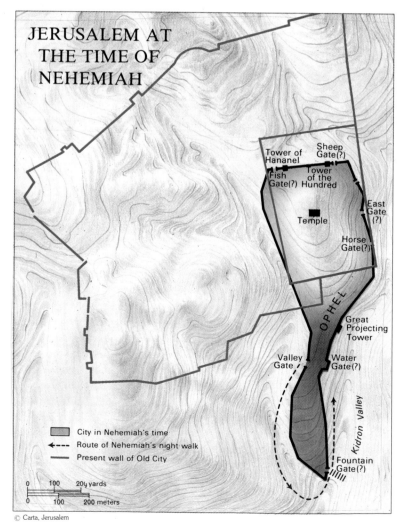

JERUSALEM AT
THE TIME OF
NEHEMIAH

Tower of Hananel, Sheep Gate(?), Fish Gate(?), Tower of the Hundred, East Gate(?), Temple, Horse Gate(?), OPHEL, Great Projecting Tower, Valley Gate, Water Gate(?), Kidron Valley, Fountain Gate(?)

City in Nehemiah's time
Route of Nehemiah's night walk
Present wall of Old City

0 100 200 yards
0 100 200 meters

© Carta, Jerusalem

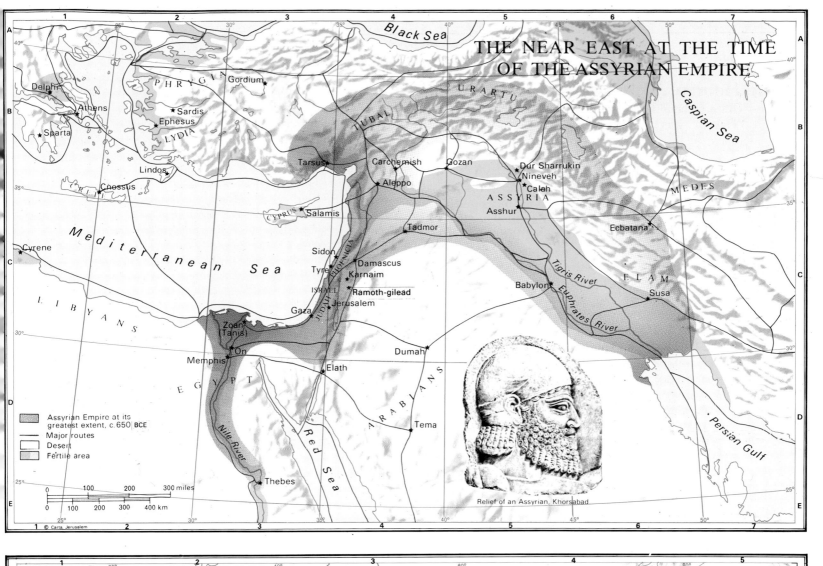

THE NEAR EAST AT THE TIME OF THE ASSYRIAN EMPIRE

Black Sea

Delphi
Athens
Sparta

PHRYGIA
Gordium
Sardis
Ephesus
LYDIA

Lindos
Cnossus
CRETE

CYPRUS
Salamis

Mediterranean Sea

LIBYANS

Cyrene

Tarsus

URARTU

TUBAL

Carchemish
Aleppo

Gozan

Dur Sharrukin
Nineveh
Calah
ASSYRIA
Asshur

MEDES

Caspian Sea

Ecbatana

Tadmor

Sidon
Tyre
PHOENICIA
Karnaim
Damascus
ISRAEL
Ramoth-gilead
Jerusalem
JUDAH
Gaza

ELAM

Babylon
Tigris River
Euphrates River
Susa

Zoan
(Tanis)
On
Memphis
Elath
EGYPT

ARABIANS

Dumah

Nile River

Red Sea

Tema

Persian Gulf

Assyrian Empire at its greatest extent, c. 650 BCE
Major routes
Desert
Fertile area

0   100   200   300 miles
0   100   200   300   400 km

Relief of an Assyrian, Khorsabad

© Carta, Jerusalem

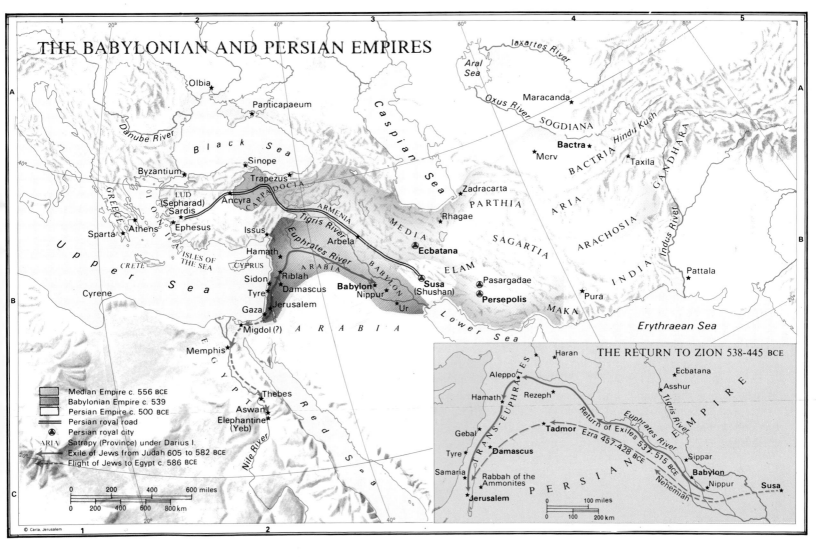

THE BABYLONIAN AND PERSIAN EMPIRES

Iaxartes River

Aral Sea

Olbia

Panticapaeum

Danube River

Black Sea

Sinope

Byzantium
Trapezus
LUD
(Sepharad)
Sardis
Ancyra
CAPPADOCIA
ARMENIA

GREECE
IONIA
Sparta
Athens
Ephesus
CRETE
ISLES OF THE SEA
CYPRUS
Cyrene

Upper Sea

Issus
Hamath
Riblah
Sidon
Damascus
Tyre
Jerusalem
Gaza
ARABIA

Migdol (?)

Memphis

Thebes
Aswan
Elephantine
(Yeb)

Nile River

Red Sea

Caspian Sea

Maracanda
SOGDIANA
Oxus River
Bactra
Merv
BACTRIA
Hindu Kush
Taxila
GANDHARA

Zadracarta
PARTHIA
ARIA
ARACHOSIA
Rhagae
MEDIA
Tigris River
Arbela
Ecbatana
ELAM
SAGARTIA
INDIA
Indus River
Pattala

Euphrates River
BABYLON
Babylon
Nippur
Ur
Susa
(Shushan)
Pasargadae
Persepolis
MAKA
Pura

Lower Sea

Erythraean Sea

Median Empire c. 556 BCE
Babylonian Empire c. 539
Persian Empire c. 500 BCE
Persian royal road
Persian royal city
Satrapy (Province) under Darius I.
Exile of Jews from Judah 605 to 582 BCE
Flight of Jews to Egypt c. 586 BCE

0   200   400   600 miles
0   200   400   600   800 km

© Carta, Jerusalem

THE RETURN TO ZION 538-445 BCE

Haran
Aleppo
Ecbatana
Asshur
Hamath
Rezeph
TRANS-EUPHRATES
Tadmor
Return of Exiles 537-515 BCE
Ezra 457-428 BCE
Euphrates River
Tigris River
Gebal
Tyre
Damascus
Samaria
Rabbah of the Ammonites
Jerusalem
Nehemiah
Babylon
Nippur
Sippar
Susa
PERSIAN EMPIRE

0   100 miles
0   100   200 km

The Hebrew Alphabet

The Hebrew lettering system consists of 22 characters. In biblical times, Hebrew was written in a script inherited from the Phoenicians. At the time of the Second Temple, the so-called "Jewish" script developed, based on the Aramaic script, from which further writing styles eventually developed.

It is believed that the early Hebrew script developed its own style in the ninth century BCE. The first appearance of the script is on the stele of King Mesha of Moab (c. 850 BCE). Other important evidence, dating from the eighth to sixth centuries BCE, was found in the Samaria ostraca (inscribed sherds), the Siloam inscription, the Arad letters, and the Lachish letters. Further light on the history of the ancient Hebrew alphabet is revealed on fragments of stone inscriptions, inscriptions on clay jars and seals from the First Temple period, a few Dead Sea Scrolls, dating from about the third century BCE, as well as single words in scrolls otherwise written in the "Jewish" script, and Hasmonean and Bar Kokhba coins. A version of this ancient Hebrew writing is still used by the Samaritans to this day.

From the seventh century BCE, Aramaic had become the official language of the Persian Empire; it was written in Aramaic script, which had Phoenician roots. In the Hellenistic period, the different countries of the former empire developed variations of this script for writing the local languages. The Jews who lived in the far-flung parts of the empire also adopted the Aramaic script, and a local variant of it developed in Judah. Passages in this modified script date from the end of the third century BCE. The "Jewish" script, also known as the Assyrian or square script, continued to develop and supersede the early Hebrew script, a process that ended in the second century CE.

From the time the "Jewish" script came into use, it was possible to distinguish separate paths of alphabet development. Scripts such as ornate square, intermediate, and cursive were distinguished for their various uses. After the destruction of the Temple and the dispersion of the Jewish people, various communities formed writing styles of their own: e.g., "Eastern," Sephardi, Ashkenazi, Italian, Yemenite, Persian, Byzantine and Karaite.

The two major document findings of the "Jewish" script and scripts which evolved from it are the Dead Sea Scrolls (c. 300 BCE to 70 CE) and the manuscripts in the Cairo *Genizah* (the earliest of which date from the eighth or ninth century CE).

With the invention of printing, certain main types became dominant and were used all over Europe. In Israel today, mainly the Ashkenazi and Sephardi script styles prevail.

Vocalization (in Hebrew, *nikkud*) is the system of signs or points accompanying the letters in Hebrew as aids for grammatically correct pronunciation. The pointing system accepted in today's Hebrew is the Tiberian system of vowel pointing, which includes 13 vowel signs placed mostly beneath the letters. Other pointing systems are the Palestinian system, which includes seven vowel signs (above and in between the letters); the simple Babylonian system, including six vowel and one half-vowel (*schwa na'*) signs (mostly above the letters); and the ornate Babylonian system, which also indicates hard and soft consonants. All these vowel systems probably developed between the seventh and mid-ninth centuries.

Transliteration Guide

Letter	Name	Latinized	Pronounced
א	aleph	'	orig. glottal stop; now silent in the middle of words if it has no vowel; otherwise pronounced according to accompanying vowel sign
ב	beth	b	
ב	bheth	v	
ג	gimel	g	hard, as in "good"
ג	ghimel	gh	orig. as gh; now like hard g
ד	daleth	d	
ד	dhaleth	dh	orig. as th in "this"; now like d
ה	hē	h	
ו	vav	v, w	(consonant)
ז	zayin	z	
ח	cheth	ch	as ch in Scottish "loch" but guttural
ט	tet	t	
י	yod	y	
ך ,כ	kaph	k	
ך ,כ	khaph	kh	as ch in Scottish "loch"
ל	lamed	l	
ם ,מ	mem	m	
ן ,נ	nun	n	
ס	samekh	s	
ע	ayin	'	strong guttural sound; now usually treated in the pronunciation like an *aleph*
פ	pē	p	
פ	phē	ph	
ץ ,צ	tzadhē	tz, ts	as ts in "tse-tse"
ק	koph	q	guttural k
ר	resh	r	
שׁ	shin	sh	as sh in "sheet"
שׂ	sin	s	
ת	tav	t	
ת	thav	th	orig. as th in "thing"; now like t

Vocalization Guide

	Vowel form	Name	Latinized	Pronounced
1) Long vowels	ָ	qamatz gadhol	ā	as a in "far"
	ֵ	tzeré	ē	as ai in "rain"
	ִי	hiriq gadhol	i	as i in "machine"
	ֹ	holam	ō	as o in "fork"
	וּ	shuruq	ū	as u in "true"
2) Short vowels	ַ	patah	a	as a in "far"
	ֶ	seghol	e	as e in "them"
	ִ	hiriq qatan	i	as i in "pin"
	ָ	qamatz qatan	o	as o in "gone"
	ֻ	qubbutz	u	as u in "put"
3) Half vowels	ְ	schwa (na')	e	as e in "agent"
	ֲ	hataph patah	a	like a very short patah
	ֱ	hataph seghol	e	like a very short seghol
	ֳ	hataph qamatz	o	like a very short qamatz qatan

Chronological Chart of the Alphabet

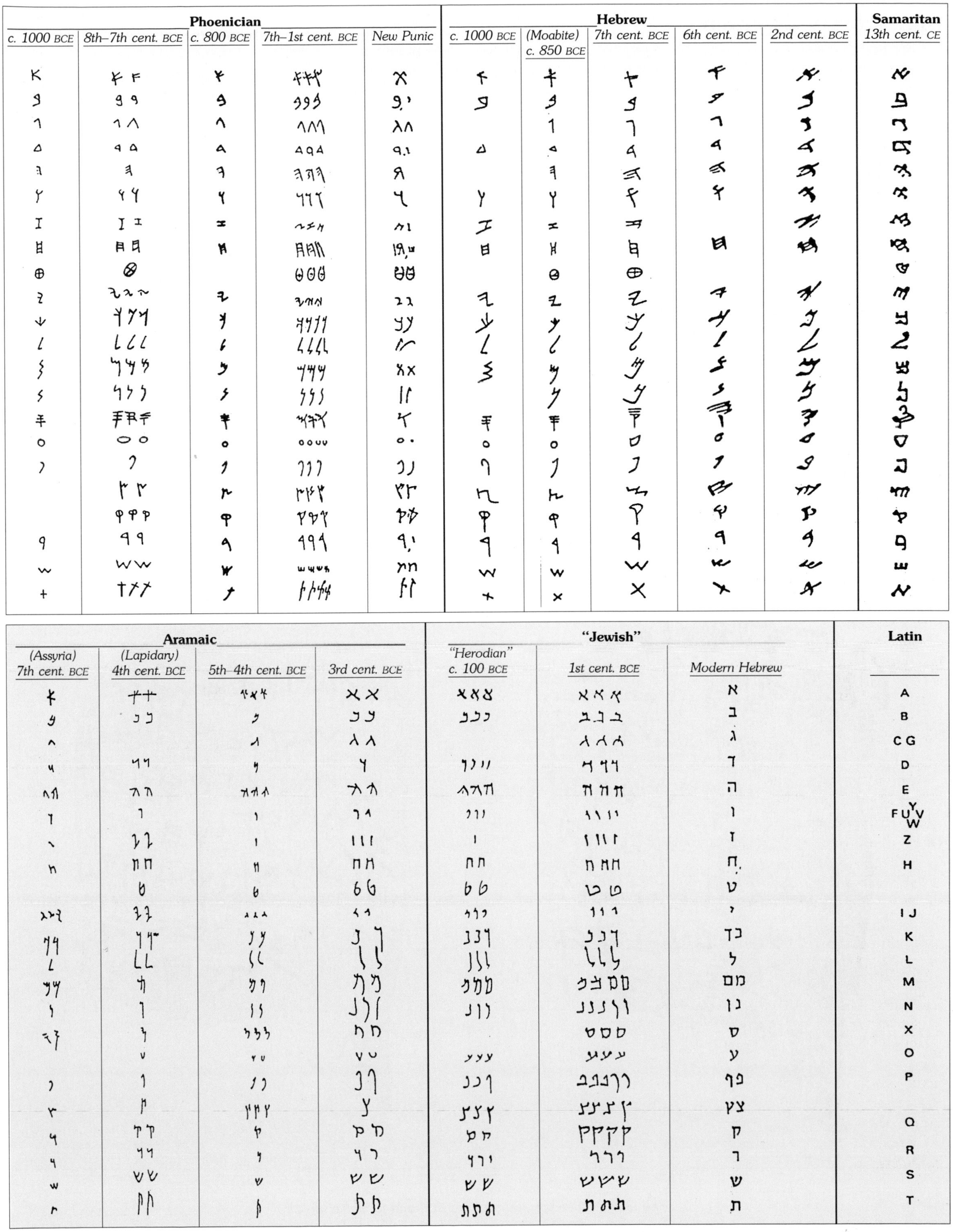
Phoenician
c. 1000 BCE
8th–7th cent. BCE
c. 800 BCE
7th–1st cent. BCE
New Punic
Hebrew
c. 1000 BCE
(Moabite) c. 850 BCE
7th cent. BCE
6th cent. BCE
2nd cent. BCE
Samaritan
13th cent. CE
Aramaic
(Assyria) 7th cent. BCE
(Lapidary) 4th cent. BCE
5th–4th cent. BCE
3rd cent. BCE
"Jewish"
"Herodian" c. 100 BCE
1st cent. BCE
Modern Hebrew
א ב ג ד ה ו ז ח ט י כך ל מם נן ס ע פף צץ ק ר ש ת
Latin
A B CG D E FUYVW Z H IJ K L M N X O P Q R S T

The Hebrew Calendar

In the Hebrew calendar, the days are reckoned from sunset to sunset, the months are calculated according to the moon, and the years according to the sun. As the lunar year consists of about 354 days and the solar year has about 365 days, the lunar cycle must be adjusted yearly to the solar calendar. Without this modification, the Jewish festivals would come 11 days earlier each year. This adjustment, first made public by the talmudic sage Hillel II in the year 359, is made by having a leap year seven times in each 19-year cycle—years 3, 6, 8, 11, 14, 17 and 19, a leap year being the intercalation of an extra month of Adar (Adar II) into the calendar.

The oldest known Hebrew calendar is the tenth-century BCE Gezer Calendar, from the start of the monarchical period. It is a calendar in which the names of the months are based on an annual cycle of agricultural activities beginning with a month of gathering, a month of sowing, a month of late sowing, one month of flax harvest, one month of barley harvest, a month of wheat harvest, a month of vine pruning or of vintage, and the month of picking or drying of figs. In the Bible, the months are generally referred to serially, Nisan being called "the first month," Iyyar "the second month," and so forth. There are four months which have special designations: Nisan (Abib—spring), Iyyar (Ziv—splendor),

Tishri (Ethanim—strength), and Marheshvan (Bul—produce). The present names of the months, which are of Akkadian, Assyrian or Babylonian origin and whose meanings are often unclear, first appear in Jewish sources during the period of the Babylonian exile, and have since been known in the following order: Tishri, Marheshvan, Kislev, Tevet, Shevat, Adar, Nisan, Iyyar, Sivan, Tammuz, Av, and Elul.

The Gezer Calendar opens with the season of gathering, but the Bible intimates clearly that the year was first counted from the month of Nisan, marking the start of the Exodus from Egypt; then for awhile the New Year (Rosh ha-Shanah) was counted from the month of Tishri and, according to the Mishnah, the 1st of Tishri was considered the New Year "for the years and for the fallow years and for the jubilee years and for the planting and for the vegetables," while the 1st of Nisan was considered as the New Year "for the kings and for the pilgrim festivals." After the destruction of the Temple, which brought about the end of royal life, Nisan was generally replaced by Tishri as the start of the New Year.

The Hebrew chronology conventionally begins with the creation of the world based on Jewish tradition. The Jewish year is calculated by adding 3760 to the civil year and, conversely, the civil year is obtained by subtracting 3760 from the Jewish year.

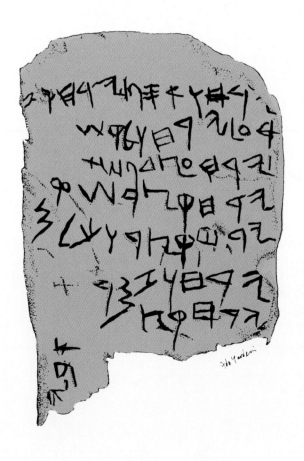

The Gezer Calendar, 10th century BCE, and facsimile (right).

Months and Festivals in the Hebrew Calendar

Hebrew month	(Civil month)	Alternative monthly order	Name source and meaning	Duration (in days)	Zodiac sign	Jewish/Israeli holidays and their dates in Hebrew calendar
1 Tishri	(Oct./Nov.)	1st month of Hebrew year, 7th from Nisan	Accadian *Tashritu* ("beginning"). In Bible called "Ethanim" (strength)	30	Libra	**1–2** Rosh ha-Shanah; **3** Fast of Gedaliah (commemorates murder of Gedaliah [II Kg. 25:25]); **10** Yom Kippur; **15–21** Sukkot; **21** Hoshana Rabbah; **22** Shmini Atzeret and Simhat Torah
2 Marheshvan	(Nov./Dec.)	2nd month from Tishri, 8th from Nisan	Accadian *Varhu samnu* ("eighth month"). Abbreviated name, Heshvan. In Bible called "Bul" (produce)	29 or 30	Scorpio	
3 Kislev	(Dec./Jan.)	3rd from Tishri, 9th from Nisan	Accadian *Kislimu, Kislivu*	29 or 30	Saggitarius	**25** Chanukkah (lasts 8 days, until 2nd or 3rd of Tevet)
4 Tevet	(Jan./Feb.)	4th from Tishri, 10th from Nisan	Accadian *Tebeitu* (perhaps "month of sinking in")	29	Capricorn	**1–3** last days of Chanukkah; **10** Fast of 10th of Tevet (commemorates the start of Nebuchadnezzar's siege on Jerusalem)
5 Shevat	(Feb./Mar.)	5th from Tishri, 11th from Nisan	Accadian *Shabatu* ("month of the beating rain")	30	Aquarius	**15** New Year for Trees
6 Adar	(Mar./Apr.)	6th from Tishri, 12th from Nisan	Accadian *Addaru* (perhaps "month of threshing")	29; in leap year — 30 in Adar I, 29 in Adar II	Pisces	**7** birth and death of Moses, marked also as Memorial Day for the Unknown Soldier; **13** Fast of Esther; **14** Purim; **15** Shushan Purim
7 Nisan	(Apr./May)	1st month of Jewish religious calendar, 7th from Tishri	Accadian *Nisannu*; in Bible called "Abib" (spring)	30	Aries	**14** Passover eve; **15–21** Passover; **16** counting of the Omer begins (continues 49 days, until Shavuot); **27** Holocaust Memorial Day
8 Iyyar	(May/June)	8th from Tishri, 2nd from Nisan	Accadian *Ayaru*; in Bible called "Ziv" (splendor)	29	Taurus	**4** Memorial Day for Israel's Fallen Soldiers; **5** Israel's Independence Day; **18** Lag ba-Omer
9 Sivan	(June/July)	9th from Tishri, 3rd from Nisan	Accadian *Simanu*	30	Gemini	**6** Shavuot (Feast of Weeks or Pentecost), commemorates Giving of the Law on Mount Sinai and Festival of the Firstfruits
10 Tammuz	(July/Aug.)	10th from Tishri, 4th from Nisan	Babylonian	29	Cancer	**17** Fast of 17th of Tammuz (commemorates breaches of the walls of Jerusalem by the Babylonians)
11 Av	(Aug./Sept.)	11th from Tishri, 5th from Nisan	Accadian *Abu*, also called "*Menahem* (= Consoler) Av"	30	Leo	**9** Fast of 9th of Av (commemorates destruction of First and Second Temples); **15** Feast of the Vineyards
12 Elul	(Oct./Nov.)	12th from Tishri, 6th from Nisan	Accadian *Elulu* ("harvest, time of harvest")	29	Virgo	

THE HOLY LAND TODAY

LEBANON

SYRIA

Damascus

Tyre · Metulla · Snir · Majdal Shams
Tibnin · Kiryat · Dan
Rosh Hanikra · Shmona · Kuneitra
Merom Golan

Nahariya · Ma'alot · Safad · Rosh Pina · GOLAN
Akko · *Galilee* · HEIGHTS · Sheikh Miskin
Carmiel
Haifa · Shefar'am · *Lake Kinneret* · Ein Gev
Kiryat Tivon · Cana Tiberias
Daliyat el-Carmel · Nazareth · Mevo Hamma
Migdal Ha'emek · Degania · Der'aa
Zichron Ya'akov · Afula · Ein
Benyamina · Harod Beit She'an · Irbid
Pardes Hanna · Umm · Jenin
Hadera · el-Fahm · Tirat Zvi · Mafrak
Netanya · Tulkarm · Tubas · Mehola
Ra'anana · Mt. · Nablus · Argaman · Jerash
Herzliya · Kalkilya · (Shechem)
Kfar Saba · *Mt.Gerizim* · Salt
Tel Aviv-Yafo · Petah · **WEST BANK** · Massu'a
Bat Yam · Tikva · Amman
Holon · Bir Zeit
Rishon Le'Zion · Lod · Ramallah
Ramla · Jericho
Rehovot · **Jerusalem** · Kalya
Yavneh · Mt. Nebo
Ashdod · Gedera · Madaba
Kiryat Malachi · Beit Shemesh · Bethlehem
Ashkelon · Kfar Etzion · Dhiban
GAZA STRIP · Kiryat Gat · Halhul
Gaza · Sderot · Dura · Hebron · Ein Gedi
Deir el-Balah · Netivot
Khan Yunis · Mishmar Hanegev
Rafah · Ofakim · Kerak
Nirim · Arad
Sheikh Zuwaid · **Beersheba** · Sodom
El-Arish · Dimona · **JORDAN**
Revivim
Yeroham · Ne'ot Hakikar
Abu Aweigila · Oron · Hatzeva · Tafila
Kusseima · *Negev*
Mitzpeh Ramon · Ein Yahav
Bir Gafgafa · Bir Hasana · Shaubak
Tzofar
Ma'an
EGYPT
Grofit
Kuntilla
Sinai · Yotvata
Thamad
Eilat
Nuweiba · Aqaba
SAUDI ARABIA

Mediterranean Sea

Dead Sea

Jordan River

Gulf of Eilat

- - - International boundary
········· Pre-1967 border
▓▓ Area of Palestinian autonomy

0 · · 20 · · 40 miles
0 · 20 · 40 · 60 km

© Carta

40